IN DEFENSE OF
LIBERTY

THE BOSTON TEA PARTY,
ITS LINEAGE *and* ITS LEGACY

James Van Ness

December, 2012

IN DEFENSE OF
LIBERTY
THE BOSTON TEA PARTY,
ITS LINEAGE *and* ITS LEGACY

JAMES VAN NESS

TATE PUBLISHING
AND ENTERPRISES, LLC

Published by Tate Publishing & Enterprises, LLC

127 E. Trade Center Terrace | Mustang, Oklahoma 73064 USA
1.888.361.9473 | www.tatepublishing.com

Tate Publishing is committed to excellence in the publishing industry. The company reflects the philosophy established by the founders, based on Psalm 68:11,

"The Lord gave the word and great was the company of those who published it."

Published in the United States of America

ISBN: 978-1-62024-482-1
HISTORY / United States / Revolutionary Period
HIS036030
12.07.11

Dedication

Nedra
and
Lynn

Table of Contents

Acknowledgments

Encouragement, help, support, and valuable criticism come from many sources.

First and foremost, my wife, Nedra, and our daughter, Lynn, were stalwart helpers, patient listeners, excellent proofreaders, and remarkably valuable critics (constructive, of course).

Lt. General (Ret.) Dave Palmer, author of, among others, *George Washington and Benedict Arnold*, devoted considerable time and applied his remarkable intellectual powers in helping me fashion what I believe is an accurate, coherent narrative.

Dr. Odie B. Faulk, Professor Emeritus of History, author of three books nominated for the Pulitzer Prize in history, lent his endorsement and encouragement. Both are greatly appreciated.

Historians always are in need of assistance from knowledge keepers.

Kathy Fulton, Director of Library Services for Temple College, was unfailing in her support, as was Todd Hively, Reference Librarian, who handled my numerous interlibrary loan requests with remarkable speed and great, good humor.

Judy Duer, Library Director for the City of Temple, and her staff provided efficient, effective support.

Denise Karimkhani, Director of Learning Resources/Librarian at the University of Mary Hardin Baylor, along with her very competent staff, proved most helpful in ferreting out resources.

Dr. Talma Botts, Chairperson of the Computer Information Services Department at Temple College, provided me with invaluable help in formatting the manuscript. Her patience, persistence, and knowledge are greatly appreciated. Mr. Pat Clune, a faculty member in the department, saved me from making some near fatal mistakes as I was being coached into twenty-first-century computer applications. Brittany Prcin, computer software specialist, carefully transformed my endnotes into computer-readable form.

In the publishing and marketing processes, sometimes a suggestion here, a point toward a previously unconsidered direction there, or an introduction to an important resource brightened the day. For one or more of these helpful gems, I thank Dick Archer, a longtime friend and confidant; Mickey White, Professor Emeritus of History at Temple College; the Honorable William A. Jones III, Mayor of Temple; Wesley A. Riddle, Chairperson of the Central Texas Tea Party; the Reverend David W. Alwine, Rector of Christ Episcopal Church; and the Honorable Dianne White Delisi, retired from the Texas House of Representatives, and currently Civilian Aide to the Secretary of the Army.

Foreword

The Tea Party phenomenon of 2009 was a tsunami crashing over the political landscape in America. It is hard to find another instance of a spontaneous, bottom-up movement having so rapid and prominent an impact on the national scene. Unless one flips back in the pages of history to December 16, 1773 to the city of Boston in the colony of Massachusetts.

There, that night, angered citizens—some disguised as Indians—boarded three ships recently arrived from London and threw overboard their cargoes of tea rather than permit parliamentary-imposed taxes to be paid on it. With just a bit of modern imagination, one can hear them chanting as they toss the perfectly good tea into the salty waters of the harbor: "Taxed Enough Already."

A big stretch, you might say. The eighteenth century is simply too far removed from the twenty-first to hold valid lessons for us today. They are not comparable eras. Anything happening back then may be interesting but is hardly likely to help us understand events in our time.

Well, let's consider:

To begin, the Revolutionary War was not actually a revolutionary war. The very word "revolution" conjures up visions of a radical upending of society, a violent break in the structure of government. Such was not the case in the American War of Independence. Power generally resided with the same elements in society before, during, and after the war. Fighting began not because Great Britain had authority over the colonies, but because the king and Parliament decided to exercise their authority in an insulting manner. Long accustomed to virtual if not actual independence, Americans rebelled. They fought for what they considered to be inalienable rights. Although the words are seldom seen together, it was a conservative revolution. It was waged against a distant government deemed to be growing too large and intrusive.

In his blockbuster pamphlet "Common Sense", Thomas Paine wrote: "government even in its best state is but a necessary evil; in its worst state an intolerable one...." Patriots devoured his words, found them compatible with their own feelings, and applauded roundly. The less government the better.

England in the 1760s faced deep financial distress. With already exorbitant internal taxes and a crushing national debt that had doubled in less than a decade, politicians frantically sought ways to squirm out of what appeared to be a looming disaster. Looking at the increasingly prosperous lands on the other side of the Atlantic, they decided to levy taxes on those British subjects even though the colonies had no representation in Parliament. A spate of tax laws followed, igniting indignant responses that often turned violent.

Surprisingly ill informed of emerging attitudes in America, London dealt with colonists' resistance peremptorily and with callousness, thus exacerbating the situation. Americans seethed at what appeared to them to be crass indifference to their concerns, particularly concerns over the challenge to what they saw as their most cherished right of all: liberty. It became their watchword. "Give me liberty or give me death!" thundered Patrick Henry. "Liberty Poles" sprang up in public places throughout the colonies. Patriots banded together in groups called "Sons of Liberty." To use a phrase in vogue today, politicians in faraway England simply "did not get it."

Those historical factors—out-of-touch and arrogant politicians, massive central debt, a growing burden of taxation, an increasingly intrusive government—aroused an inherently conservative and essentially grassroots reaction all across the thirteen colonies. That truth might suggest parallels between then and now, which could indeed help us assess the significance of the modern Tea Party movement. At the very least, we should question those who would arbitrarily label as irrelevant those past events.

In the months leading up to the national elections of 2010, critics belittled the Tea Party movement; in the shocking aftermath of the election, many of those same critics turned to denouncing it. The unavoidable fact, however, is that the movement changed the calculus of electoral politics in the country.

Still, questions remain. Will it endure, or is it a one-act play? Is it genuinely conservative? Does it have deep roots in our history? Does it merit the linkage by name to the Boston Tea Party?

James Van Ness, a respected scholar of the American Revolutionary era and an insightful observer of the current national political scene, undertakes with commendable authenticity to suggest some answers to those questions. He does so by telling the story of the widespread American reaction to London's ill-fated attempt to impose yet another tax, this one on imported tea. Importantly, he provides context for the reaction, showing how arguments in the decade before led inexorably to the confrontation in Boston Harbor and how activities afterward led, in a mere two and a half years, to the Declaration of Independence. In doing so, he provides pertinent grist for evaluating the current Tea Party movement.

He leaves the evaluation to each of his readers. However, before diving into the book itself, take note of his final words, suggesting that "these eighteenth-century developments have relevance to twenty-first century movements."

Reflect on them as you read the fascinating story of the Boston Tea Party and its lineage its and legacy.

Dave Palmer
Lt. Gen. (Ret.), US Army
Author of *George Washington and Benedict Arnold*

Preface

During spring 2009, around tax time, protest groups sprang up in various parts of the nation. Though having independent, local origins, they chose the same two words as part of their organization's name: Tea Party, implying they were spiritual descendants of those involved in the original Boston Tea Party.

Liberal pundits almost immediately attacked members of these new organizations that seemed to be advancing a conservative economic and political agenda. A favorite criticism was that these twenty-first-century protesters were ignorant of American history: there was, the pundits said, no relationship between the issues motivating the 1773 Boston Tea Party participants and issues motivating the 2009 participants.

No connection between local groups forming in 1773 and those 2009 local, loosely connected groups? Really?

Early in my professional career, I spent some time studying the American Revolutionary era, but memory is not infallible. So, possibly unlike the pundits, I went back to study again the pre-Revolutionary Era, starting, of course, with the Boston Tea Party and the events and arguments preceding it.

Would I find that today's pundits had it right: there really was no justification for the new groups to claim ties to the original Tea Party? Or were there indeed interesting comparisons between events in the 1770s and those unfolding in the twenty-first century?

Answers to these questions should be found in the following pages. They contain the story of colonists' activities—economic, political, religious, and intellectual—from the end of the French and Indian War through the adoption of the Declaration of Independence, and featuring events and arguments immediately preceding the Boston Tea Party of December 16, 1773.

There is yet another matter that is not discussed in the narrative but that may be implied from it.

In the time since modern tea party groups became active in the American political process, I have heard comments to the effect that the revolutionary formation of the American Republic was simply a struggle for colonists to cut their bonds to Britain for selfish reasons. The goals were relatively narrow. There is no evidence, some of today's commentators say, that those involved were doing more than that. Yet since those Revolutionary times, claims have been made that patriots were involved in something greater: that they were establishing a beacon for freedom and liberty to shine around the world, a model nation for others to emulate. This, I now heard, was not the case. America was founded as simply one nation among many, with no special mission and certainly no claim to be an inspiration to oppressed people elsewhere.

Having a prejudice in favor of studying history, I went to one of our nation's great leaders, Abraham Lincoln, to see what he had to say on the matter.

During the interim between Lincoln's election to the presidency and his taking office, several states in the Deep South declared their separation from the nation. Of course, Lincoln worried about the possible consequence of those states' action and whether it might mean the death of the nation as that nation had developed over the preceding three-quarters of a century. He spoke about his concerns to the New Jersey State Senate some three weeks before he took the oath of office.

Lincoln recalled reading, as a youth, of General Washington's Christmastime attack on the Hessian troops at Trenton in 1776, and the painful experiences Washington's soldiers endured following the victory. Lincoln then told the New Jersey senators of his thoughtful reaction to this dramatic story:

> Boy even though I was ... [I realized] there must have been something more than common that those men struggled for. I am exceedingly anxious that that thing which they struggled for; that something even more than National Independence; that something that held out a great promise to all the people of the world to all time to come; I am exceedingly anxious that this Union, the Constitution, and the liberties of the people shall be perpetuated in accordance with the original idea for which that struggle was made, and I shall be most happy indeed if I shall be an humble instrument in the hands of the Almighty, and of this, his almost chosen people, for perpetuating the object of that great struggle.[1]

So, was Abraham Lincoln right: that Washington and other leaders—military and civilian, national and local—involved in overturning British rule and transforming the colonies into an independent nation believed they were fighting for more than their personal freedom, for creating a government and society that would serve as a beacon of liberty to the world? Or are those current commentators right who maintain that the American patriots were simply pursuing their own selfish ends?

The pages that follow will not answer the question but will provide historical information that may help the reader decide to his or her satisfaction.

Prologue

"I can't but consider it an Epocha in History."

John Adams

They looked like windrows in the moonlight. Yet had people stepped on one of those rows, they would have found themselves sinking through piles of dried leaves, some three feet of salt water, on down into the harbor mud.

Non-participants observed from dry land.

A large, quiet crowd was watching men spill tens of thousands of pounds of tea—good Bohea tea, much in demand by Boston mistresses—over the sides of the ships Dartmouth and Eleanor and the brig Beaver into Boston harbor. So much tea was being dumped into the harbor it sometimes piled up and over the ships' gunwales. As the work crews pushed it away and the tide rearranged the clumps, the "windrows" developed.

The British commander of warships in Boston harbor watched from a nearby house where he was a guest. Oblivious of the admiral's presence, local patriots dumped the contents of over three hundred tea chests into that harbor. The admiral did nothing to stop the destruction. He could have worked in concert with the commander of British troops housed on Castle William Island to thwart patriot efforts. They would have moved against the crowd if Governor Hutchinson had asked for their assistance. At that time, the military acted only after a senior civilian official sought their help. Such respect by Britain's military for civilian authority was not long to last.

That evening, December 16, 1773, Governor Hutchinson was taking his leisure in his country home in Milton, seven miles outside Boston. He left his Boston office and home when he learned that a large crowd would gather to discuss the issue of dutied tea. He preferred to stay away from what he considered to be an illegal mob.

Hutchinson had tasted violence's gall when a mob attacked his house eight years previously. He did not want to be present should another mob build up a violent anger against him as it had in 1765, when it virtually destroyed his house and its contents.

Earlier that day of December 16, William Rotch, whose family owned the ship Dartmouth, had gone to Milton and made a desperate appeal to the governor for permission to return the ship, with the tea in its hold, to London. Governor Hutchinson refused, arguing that under British law the tea must be unloaded and the three-pence-per-pound tax paid on it. He might have taken this position in order to protect the interest of family members who were among those the East India Company had selected to handle tea sales in Massachusetts.

Whatever Hutchinson's motivation, he conveniently forgot that colonial governors could take action they thought appropriate in an emergency. He also conveniently overlooked the advice his executive council had given him about the tea consignment. Members of the council declared the tea's landing (and therefore having the tax paid) to be "inconsistent with the declared sentiment of both houses" of the legislature. While not explicitly urging him to authorize the return of the as yet untaxed tea to England, councilors made plain their unstated recommendation that the governor do so.[2]

Why was Rotch so desperate? And why was the large Meeting House crowd so eager to hear the results of his interview with Governor Hutchinson?

Because under British law, a ship registering its contents with the customs office had twenty days to complete its unloading and pay any duties due on goods it had brought to the port. The Dartmouth's captain had recorded its cargo with the customs office twenty days previously. If Rotch did not pay the tea tax and unload the tea before midnight, come December 17, customs officials would confiscate the tea and claim it for the government. He believed the local patriots would not agree to his paying the duty, and therefore he might owe the East India Company several thousand British pounds sterling for the confiscated tea, which had shipped the consignment on his vessel. Owners of the other two vessels also faced daunting penalties if the tea were not unloaded and the tax paid within their respective twenty-day periods.

When Rotch returned to Boston and told an overflow crowd in the Old South Meeting House about the governor's response, several patriots expressed outrage. Then Sam Adams, or one of the other leading patriots located near the podium, gave a signal, and three teams of men, mostly of the "middling sort" and probably including the artisan and patriot Paul Revere, as well as many other artisans and workmen, descended on the three vessels.

The result was, as they say, "history."

That Tea Party history will play out here. It will be preceded by some major political and economic events. Colonial religious and ideological developments that influenced, perhaps shaped, patriot responses to parliamentary actions follow.

When combined, these events and developments led to the Boston Tea Party. Following those stories will be the British government's reactions to rejections of duted tea shipments sent to Boston, New York, Philadelphia, and Charleston. Those British reactions prompted strong, sustained patriot responses—political, ideological, and military—culminating in America's Declaration of Independence, the first of our nation's enduring statements of principles.

Remember as you read, just as someone once said, "elections matter," there is an even more consequential dictate: ideas matter.

Among those, in the following pages the thought that "liberty" is both an idea and a value which people of all stations, including "the middling sort," prize dearly will be put to the test. One thesis of the book is that liberty is a prize people will fight to gain or defend: through words, through independent and concerted action, and when absolutely necessary, through the outpouring of their blood, so that those who come after will enjoy the resultant spirit of freedom.

I

After a Glorious Military Victory, Parliament Expects the Colonies to Pay the Piper

Coupled with a directive from London in 1753 to protect the colony's western borders and order any French interlopers to leave, Virginia's governor received an ominous warning. If the French refused to leave, he was to "enforce by arms (if necessary)" their removal.

Early in 1754, the governor ordered twenty-one-year-old militia Lieutenant Colonel George Washington to take all the soldiers under his command (159) and push French and Indian forces out of the Ohio valley. Washington, who picked up additional men on his way west, tried to fulfill the governor's orders but learned the French and their Indian allies vastly outnumbered his forces. Instead of attacking the enemy, he constructed Fort Necessity, located some miles to the east of the French camp. Being naive to siege warfare, Washington built the fort in a meadow surrounded by wooded hills. Those hills provided the attackers with ideal cover.

On July 3, 1754, a French detachment, more than double the number of able-bodied men than Washington could muster, attacked and captured the beleaguered Virginians.[3]

So began the French and Indian War in America, and the Seven Years' War in Europe and Asia. It was the culmination of a half-century of intermittent warfare between France and Britain. Almost nine years later, the conflict ended with the Peace of Paris. One article in that treaty acknowledged that France ceded all of Canada to Britain, ending France's involvement in North American colonization; in another article, Spain ceded Florida to Britain, thus giving Britain control of the entire continent east of the Mississippi River.[4]

Thousands of American colonists participated in the fighting, and several colonial legislatures appropriated large sums to aid the British during the war, while others ignored the contest. But once the colonists learned a favorable peace would be struck, an outpouring of British nationalism flowed forth in the form of letters to newspapers, pamphlets, and sermons. Americans were proud of their part in Britain's military victory, and they professed their loyalty to Britain and its extensive empire, the largest empire in world history, many claimed.

Even before the battle smoke cleared, Puritan minister Jonathan Mayhew envisioned a peace that would lead to America becoming: "a mighty empire (I do not mean an independent one) in numbers little inferior to the greatest in Europe, and in felicity to none." But Americans could not achieve this alone. They would need divine help: "the Lord [will be]…as a wall of fire round about, and the glory in the midst of her! O happy country! happy kingdom!"[5]

Yet, with peace, Parliament was forced to face the realities of governance but chose politics of expediency. That politics ignored or brushed aside colonists' professions of loyalty to Britain.

In England, despite heavy taxation during the war, the nation faced a severe fiscal problem. Prior to the war, Britain had an astounding debt of seventy-five million pounds sterling; when peace returned in 1763, that debt had grown to 146 million pounds sterling, almost double its excessively high prewar debt. And this was on top of those heavy taxes, which raised about ten million pounds sterling annually. Added to this were the new costs of maintaining an expanded empire and prominent government supporters bringing pressure to reduce taxes.

Parliament was in a bind.

Then along came a government decision to keep a standing army of ten thousand troops in the American colonies. Many colonists worried about this. True, British troops sometimes were stationed among them in response to a military crisis, but there had been no standing army in the colonies during peacetime while France controlled Canada and Spain Florida.

Why now?

Cabinet leaders and members of the parliamentary majority offered facile rationales but no solid reasons for keeping a permanent military force among the colonists.

Then Parliament generated new worries for the colonists. The ministry hit on two plans not only to pay for the upkeep of Britain's army in America but also to fund other governmental expenses in the colonies.

First was the Sugar Act of 1764, which largely rewrote the old Molasses Act of 1733. That act, passed at the behest of plantation owners in the British West Indies, had levied a heavy duty on molasses imported into the colonies from non-British West Indies islands. The rationale was that the colonies should buy all their molasses (most of which went to making rum for export) from the British islands. Yet those British islands could not come close to supplying the colonies' needs. Since the tax was so high colonists could not pay it and still turn a profit, they conveniently ignored it and smuggled molasses into their ports. Colonial merchants were able to do this in part because men appointed as customs commissioners were prominent Englishmen who drew their salaries as a "sinecure" and therefore remained in England. They pocketed most of the "salary" and then appointed "deputy" customs collectors, at a minimal salary, to go to the colonies and collect the duties. Those deputies received such meager salaries they were easily bribed to look the other way when a molasses ship from a foreign island was due in port.[6]

Under the Sugar Act of 1764, duties on foreign molasses were cut in half. Customs collectors were no longer given the luxury of hiring substitutes but were required to take the posts themselves. They also received new legal tools to improve their effectiveness in ferreting out smugglers. Vigorous enforcement followed.

The tax, which was designed to regulate trade, targeted merchants and ship owners but generated burdens beyond them to many working people. This simply exacerbated financial problems many faced due to a postwar depression that had swept across the colonies. Soon, opposition came from colonial legislatures. Eight legislative bodies sent petitions to England complaining about the disruption in trade and the loss of business the Sugar Act's taxes and regulations were generating. This was a new form of political action and set the stage for much that was to come. For the first time, British merchants and government officials felt the sting of Americans' criticism.[7]

Parliament ignored the colonists' petitions and continued enforcing the Sugar Act. Yet that act's taxes did not generate the amount of net revenue from the colonies that Parliament had in mind.

So they adopted a new measure: the Stamp Tax.

In 1765, the cabinet pushed Parliament to levy taxes in the colonies on commercial and legal transactions as well as on the sale of newspapers and some other items. This was the Stamp Act, and it placed the first ever direct tax on the colonists.

Although members of the Treasury Department had been gathering information on possible American reaction to a stamp tax for several months, and spent considerable time drafting a Stamp Act, they handled neither matter well.

Thomas Whatley, Secretary of the Treasury, had corresponded with some prominent men in America, both private businessmen and government officials, on the tax issue. He chose to ignore their warnings that such a measure would be met with strong criticism. Jared Ingersoll, a Connecticut merchant and a person loyal to the king, said New Englanders were "filled with the most dreadful apprehensions from such a step's taking place." Whatley's response was that Americans would just have to learn to swallow those fears, for Britain needed new sources of revenue. He wrote to John Temple, a senior customs official in New England, who had argued such a tax would not be "prudent," suggesting treasury officials in London would "not give entire credit to all the objections that are raised on your side of the water."[8]

Despite seeking colonists' advice about the tax issue, Whatley brushed aside the warnings his colonial correspondents had offered. According to one historian who studied the matter closely, Whatley "surmounted the obstacle by pretending that it did not exist." He drafted a stamp bill, which he submitted for a departmental review in early December 1764. Eventually Parliament passed it on March 22, 1765. Yet even while the House of Commons was considering the matter, officials in various government offices read the act and raised questions as to how it might be implemented in the colonies. For example, when a former Attorney General for the Crown was asked to review the draft stamp bill, he suggested that as it was written the only offense for which one could be charged for violating the act was that of forgery, and that such a charge could be brought in any colonial court of law, rather than in a designated court. Yet parliamentary leaders made no changes in the bill to address either problem.

After the act became law, no one in London seemed to know how revenue collected from the sale of the stamps would be handled. Nor had anyone designated stamp agents for each colony, determined how their bonds were to be secured, what they were to be paid, or how the taxes they collected would be transferred to officials and army personnel whose salaries were to be paid from that income.[9]

In implementing this tax policy, Parliament intended to make clear that it ruled the empire just as it ruled the British nation. Perhaps the fumbling going on with respect to Stamp Act details gave an inkling of how effectively Parliament did, indeed, rule the empire.

British leaders soon learned that colonists were arguing they could be taxed only by their colonial legislators. The prime minister and his supporters scoffed at the idea. They held that colonies existed in law based on a royal charter. So, too, did English municipalities. No alderman in Bristol or Leeds would dare challenge Parliament's right to levy taxes on municipal residents. In law, parliamentary leaders argued, colonies were inferior to Parliament. The colonists would just have to learn to accept taxation and regulation.

Americans responded by calling a Stamp Act Congress. Delegates from nine colonies, chosen mostly by colonial legislatures, and therefore men who held moderate to conservative views, announced that the Stamp Act illegally took Americans' property without their consent. Delegates framed a petition to the king, with copies to the House of Commons and House of Lords. In the petition they noted that such "internal" taxes as the Stamp Act created were unconstitutional because "it is inseparably essential to the Freedom of a People, and the undoubted Right of Englishmen, that no Taxes be imposed on them but with their own Consent, given personally, or by their Representatives."

After stating that American colonists could not be represented in Parliament because of the distance involved, delegates to the Stamp Act Congress reiterated their position that the Stamp Act threatened their liberty by violating their rights as Englishmen: "That the only Representatives of the People of these Colonies, are Persons chosen therein by themselves, and that no Taxes ever have been, or can be Constitutionally imposed on them, but by their respective Legislature."[10]

At about the same time, several colonial legislatures sent their own petitions to London. Two of these, from Pennsylvania and Massachusetts, went beyond the Congress's appeal to rights of Englishmen by claiming exemption from parliamentary taxation on the basis of "natural rights." The Massachusetts petition stated: "That there are certain essential rights of the British constitution of government, which are founded in the law of God and nature, and are the common rights of mankind," which included protection from unlawful seizure of an individual's property without his consent, or the consent of his duly elected representative. These more general claims of exemption from parliamentary taxation based on natural law, though in the minority, gave support to as yet a novel theoretical argument: the colonies should be independent of any parliamentary control.[11]

While debates on political theory were under way, patriots in several colonies used intimidation or force to "persuade" those the British Government eventually had appointed as stamp distributors to resign their post.

Bostonians were especially forward in the use of physical force to secure their aims and demonstrate their wrath.

The "riots" that occurred in Boston which led to the local Stamp Act Distributor's resignation were no spontaneous, happenstance events. Apparently in response to news of Parliament passing the Stamp Act, a group of middle-class men began meeting as a social club around the middle of 1765. They met in a local distillery, Chase and Speakman's, on Hanover Square, and called themselves "The Loyal Nine." Included were two distillers, two "brasiers" (presumably braziers or brass workers), a printer, a painter, a merchant, and a jeweler. The occupation of the other member is not known. What is clear is that none of the prominent patriots, either within the lower house of the legislature or among the local political and propaganda leaders, were "members," though Sam Adams is thought to have been a frequent guest at their meetings. John Adams and some other notable patriots also attended one or more of their meetings, but the members all were men of the "middling" or "meaner" sort.

One man who must have been an invited guest at several meetings in July or August was Ebenezer McIntosh. A shoemaker, he was much better known as the captain of the South End Mob. For some years, McIntosh had led his forces against the North End Mob on Pope's Day, or Guy Fawkes Day, November 5. (It was on that date in 1605 that a plot to blow up Parliament and replace the legislature with a Catholic government was discovered in London and quashed.)

Those friendly Guy Fawkes Day clashes in Boston, which always ended with several members sustaining serious injuries, had reached a crescendo the previous year, 1764. "Captain" McIntosh masterminded a thoroughgoing victory for his South End minions. Now, members of the Loyal Nine persuaded him to organize a new mob, merging those from North and South, which would be used to defend American liberty by seeing that no one in the government dared try to enforce the Stamp Act. At the same time, Loyal Nine Club members apparently spoke quietly with political leaders who were of the patriot persuasion, securing their unofficial acceptance of the Club's action plan. In Boston, men of the middle class were becoming major patriot leaders and organizers.

On August 14, someone—or group—hung two effigies in the center of Boston: one representing Andrew Oliver, the man reputed to be the local Stamp Tax Distributor, and the other, a boot representing Lord Bute, a former British prime minister. Many colonists thought the Stamp Act was Lord Bute's brainchild. He was one of the most hated men in England (and, presumably, in America as well). Lieutenant Governor Thomas Hutchinson, who also held the post of Chief Justice, ordered the sheriff to remove the effigies. Later that afternoon, the sheriff told Governor Bernard his men refused to try and remove the effigies because they feared for their lives.

There is reason to believe the sheriff's deputies did, in fact, fear for their own well-being. That evening McIntosh led a large mob to Kilby Street, where the stamp distributor-to-be, Andrew Oliver, recently had constructed a building which many in town assumed would be headquarters for the sale of stamped paper. Members of the mob knew what to do. After razing the building, they celebrated by "stamping" and then burning the Oliver effigy. In quick order they moved to his house, a handsome mansion. When they finished with the yard, garden, and, of course, the house and its contents, Oliver, who had frantically moved with his family to a nearby friend's house, must have known he could not, with safety, hold on to the post of stamp distributor. The next day, he resigned.

The Boston story did not end with Andrew Oliver's punishment and resignation. During the mob's destruction of the Oliver house, Lieutenant Governor/Chief Justice Hutchinson, who was not nearly as prudent as the governor, went there, with the sheriff by his side. Presumably Hutchinson intended to order the mob to disperse. Before he could do so, he and the sheriff felt the mob's sting as a shower of rocks sent them packing. But McIntosh and the mob apparently were insulted by Hutchinson's interference, for about two weeks later they separated into two groups and warmed up by severely damaging the home of a man who allegedly had written officials in London criticizing merchants who opposed the Stamp Act. They also wreaked havoc on the home of the comptroller of customs. Then the two mobs merged and went to Hutchinson's home. They spent the remainder of the night demolishing what some considered one of the grandest houses in Boston, along with its rich furnishings and lovely surroundings.

The next day, the sheriff arrested Ebenezer McIntosh, who put up no resistance. Word went out to customs employees that if McIntosh were tried and if a mob then should take vengeance on the Customs House, no one would defend those inside. Customs officials accordingly asked the sheriff to release McIntosh, and soon mob organizer McIntosh was back making shoes in the South End.[12]

News of the two mob attacks in Boston spread down the coast, as local newspapers picked up the stories and reprinted them. These were followed by letters commenting on the events. Some thanked the Boston group for showing them how to block implementation of the Stamp Act: by forcing the colonial stamp collectors to resign, leaving government with no means of distributing stamped paper. Some commented on the attack on stamp distributor Oliver's office and home, justifying it on the basis of the British government's refusal to consider formal appeals colonial legislatures had made for a redress of grievances. When responsible magistrates act irresponsibly (as the patriots maintained Parliament had done by ignoring appeals to rescind the Stamp Act), then direct action to redress a legitimate public grievance could be taken. Not so, though, with the vicious attack on the Hutchinson household, and the lesser assaults on others. There was no public grievance involved in that attack, and those responsible should be condemned. So, patriots were looking at events with a critical eye and were willing to condemn what they considered unwarrantable excesses while at the same time defending those which transpired only after conventional methods for seeking relief had been tried and failed.[13]

When the stamped paper arrived in a colonial port, no one was at the dock to receive and distribute it, but colony-by-colony, this solid resistance did not result directly from Stamp Act Congress pronouncements. Instead, it stemmed from relatively small, economically heterogeneous groups of "Sons of Liberty" organized in towns, counties, and cities that took the initiative to resist Stamp Act dictates in concrete terms. Their primary tactic was organizing boycotts of purchases of British goods. In Boston, the Loyal Nine Club morphed into a somewhat larger Sons of Liberty organization during or shortly after the mob actions.

The name Sons of Liberty came from a comment a member of Parliament, Colonel Isaac Barre, made during a speech in the House of Commons. Many colonial newspapers reprinted his speech. Colonel Barre had been on active duty in America during the French and Indian War. He ridiculed a disparaging comment Charles Townshend had made concerning the colonists' bravery in battle. Barre noted the American colonists were "the most formidable of any people upon the face of God's earth…the sons of liberty [carry a] spirit of freedom. …"[14]

While these Sons of Liberty organizations were new in name, in many cases, as in Boston, they had existed in other forms, often for quite different purposes. The nucleus of several Sons groups came from Masonic lodges; members of local churches organized others; at least one had at its core a volunteer fire department; another, a volunteer militia artillery unit; social clubs formed the basis of others.

Most of the Sons' organizations recruited individuals from varied walks of life, with nearly all of them including a few "men of substance and standing," in addition to many of the "middling sort." In these organizations, leadership devolved on those with special talents, rather than falling necessarily to the most prominent members. This was a relatively new tendency in social intercourse. A few decades earlier, men of "substance" would have expected those of a lower social/economic class to give deference to them. And, indeed, outside of essential business communication, the "middling sort" would not have expected to interact with their "betters" in any voluntary association. As will be seen later, a period of religious enthusiasm that began around 1740 stimulated a groundswell of activity for the two decades following, which changed much of peoples' outlook toward themselves and toward each other.

Showing their pride, the Sons groups readily publicized their meetings and posted their resolutions. They also organized correspondence committees to communicate with likeminded groups in other parts of their colony, as well as those in other colonies. When an unknown person (who was presumed to be a government spy) intercepted and read one of the letters, several persons took it upon themselves to travel north and south to arrange a safe, unofficial mail service. After that, letters seemed to reach their intended destinations without outside interference.

Sons took action against crown and colonial officials to preserve their freedoms as they defined those freedoms. They saw that area merchants and shopkeepers honored the boycott of British goods in opposition to the Stamp Act. When rumors floated through the northeast that British troops were headed for New York to enforce the Stamp Act, members of Sons of Liberty organizations in that colony entered into a formal written agreement with Sons in Connecticut to come to each other's aid in the event military conflict broke out. Clearly, the men in these groups took seriously their commitment to protecting American liberty.[15]

After a few weeks of indecision following the November 1 date Parliament had set for enforcing the Stamp Act, colonial commercial interests pressured local courts to reopen without the use of "required" stamped paper. This action to force government agencies that affected normal business to reopen without stamped paper had both practical and theoretical goals. Practically, those involved in commercial activity did not want to lose business as a result of closed agencies. Theoretically, patriots wanted to show that British rules did not apply to the colonies. Had they waited for Parliament to rescind the Stamp Act, that would have implied recognition of parliamentary power over them.

When a customs official in North Carolina confiscated ships for not having stamped clearance papers, a local Sons of Liberty group rectified the situation. Newspapers quickly resumed publication, without stamps.

Colonial rejection of Parliament's Stamp Act created another problem for the king. For seven years following William Pitt's departure as prime minister in 1761, young King George III could not find a strong, stable leader of the government who also was loyal to him. So it was during the Stamp Act standoff that the king replaced one leader with yet another man who could barely muster a working coalition.

A new parliamentary leader responded to the colonists' economic pressure by rescinding the Stamp Act in 1766. At the same time Parliament passed the Declaratory Act. That measure asserted Parliament's supremacy over the colonies "in all cases whatsoever."[16]

Not everyone in Parliament agreed with the Declaratory Act. When members of the House of Lords debated the bill, a prominent peer rose to object. He called the bill: "absolutely illegal, contrary to the fundamental laws of this constitution." That constitution, he said, was "grounded on the eternal and immutable laws of nature." One aspect of those immutable laws was that "taxation and representation are inseparably united... ." American colonists were to repeat this argument a thousand times over during the succeeding decade, coupled with the observation that colonists were not, and could not be, represented in Parliament.[17]

In its euphoria over defeating the Stamp Act's tax, colonists blithely ignored the Declaratory Act as being of no consequence. Members of Parliament, though, held fast to that act as the cornerstone of the institution's relations with, and control over, the colonies.

The Stamp Act's repeal left the British government with a significant financial problem: continuing heavy debt payments from the war, and the cost of administering the colonies without any significant tax revenues coming from those colonies.

Taxes within Britain were generating about ten million pounds sterling annually. But interest on its huge debt required five million pounds. Routine domestic costs ate up the other five million, leaving nothing to pay for administrative and military costs associated with running the empire.

What to do?

"Champaign Charley" Townshend took time out from his notorious nighttime carousing to accept the post of Chancellor of the Exchequer, or tax collector and disburser, under yet another new ministry. Unfortunately, the man now serving as prime minister really was too sick to lead a government effectually, but he had too large an ego to refuse the king's request that he form one.

Chancellor of the Exchequer Townshend recalled being in Parliament in February 1766, when Benjamin Franklin had been questioned about colonial views on the Stamp Tax. At that time Franklin made a clear distinction between "internal" taxes, such as the Stamp Tax, as designed to raise revenue, and "external" taxes, such as the Sugar Act, the purpose of which was to regulate trade. Internal taxes, Franklin had said, were illegal and unconstitutional because only the colonists' elected representatives could take property away from citizens through taxation, and the colonists were not represented in Parliament. On the other hand, he believed Parliament did have legitimate authority to levy import duties on the colonists as part of its responsibility to regulate trade within the empire. He stressed that Parliament could only impose external taxes for regulating the empire's trade and not design them to raise revenue.[18]

That was in 1766. With Charles Townshend leading the way in 1768, Parliament decided to ignore Franklin's restrictive definition of legitimate external taxes.

Just as many in America ignored the importance of Parliament's 1766 Declaratory Act claiming its supremacy over the colonies, so in 1768 Townshend ignored Franklin's stipulation that "external taxes" only were legitimate if their purpose was the regulation of trade (which the Molasses Act of 1733 clearly was, however poorly it was enforced, along with the revisions of that act in the Sugar Act of 1764).

Townshend said external taxes were any import duties levied on the colonies, and Parliament was free to decide the purposes to which the income from those duties was put. If Parliament wished to use import duties to raise revenue, the colonists would have no grounds on which to object since, in his eyes, these duties amounted to "external taxes."

Over the prime minister's feeble objections, Townshend persuaded Parliament to impose a series of duties on goods shipped to the colonies. These Townshend Duties were on glass, lead, paper, paint, and tea. The Townshend Act's preamble further snubbed colonists' arguments about external taxes being legitimate only if they were designed to regulate trade by stating specifically that the duties were to raise revenue.

Parliament was putting into action what it expressed in theory in the Declaratory Act: Parliament was supreme in the empire in all matters of law and taxes.

Though the colonies were suffering through a postwar recession at the time, many patriots put long-term defense of principle over short-term economic distress. While some important economic leaders objected, patriots again organized a boycott of British goods. One result of this was that violence occurred in several seaports, including Boston.

Back in London, the king removed yet another prime minister and replaced him with yet another ineffectual leader.

Though the reason he did so is not clear, the new prime minister dropped all Townshend Duties except the tea tax. His successor as prime minister, Lord North, continued that tax, but with most of the Townshend Duties gone, the American boycott collapsed.

Yet before these changes took place, colonists raised more Cain.

A furious and intemperate verbal battle arose between Massachusetts Governor Francis Bernard and the lower house of the legislature in March 1768. The popular newspaper Boston Gazette joined the fray, publishing a vituperative letter denigrating the governor. Bernard asked his Lieutenant Governor/Chief Justice Thomas Hutchinson to secure a grand jury indictment against the publishers for libel, which Hutchinson attempted. When Hutchinson asked the sitting grand jury for an indictment against the publishers, the grand jurors rejected his charge. Hutchinson complained in a letter that he wished he could quash the "absurd notion of the liberty of the press."[19]

Later in 1768, Boston was the scene of more mob violence, this in reaction to the Townshend Duties and to vigorous enforcement of the customs acts. Reports of these assaults, following on previous news of extensive mob violence the Stamp Act had stimulated, prompted the cabinet to order British troops posted to the city.

Almost as soon as the troops arrived, minor skirmishes erupted between soldiers and Bostonians. And despite the cabinet's intention that the troops' presence would intimidate Boston's rabble rousers, the Boston Gazette conducted a campaign against both the troops and Governor Bernard until Bernard gave up the ghost and returned to London. Lieutenant Governor Hutchinson succeeded Bernard as Governor. Bernard's departure did not solve the problem of the troops' presence in the city.[20]

On March 5, 1770, a small mob harassed soldiers on duty in the center of town. Apparently fearing for their lives, several soldiers fired into the crowd, killing five men. Boston Sons of Liberty described this as "The Boston Massacre." The term "Boston Massacre" became a symbol for American resistance.

Reacting to the "Massacre," the Boston town meeting demanded that the new Massachusetts governor, Thomas Hutchinson, order removal of all British troops from the town center to Castle William in the harbor. With the governor's council's ready concurrence, Hutchinson gave the order. In England, members of Parliament condemned mob action in Boston. Though John Adams successfully defended in court the officer and men charged with murder, parliamentary leaders saw the event as additional evidence that Boston was a den of sedition.

Normal commercial activities returned to the colonies following the end of the Townshend boycott. Colonists involved in all aspects of trade, from farmers practicing commercial agriculture to shipbuilders to merchants handling goods shipped from and to Britain, prayed for peaceful times. Those dedicated to agitating for American liberty fell into a funk.

Even though conflicts continued between naval officers or customs officials and coastal schooners or local residents, the contests generated attention only in the general area around the strife. While some of these disagreements led to injuries or death, not even the best propagandist could transform them into a major conflict between liberty and tyranny.

Until a Rhode Island incident started a patriotic avalanche.

Patriot spirits in New England received a boost in 1772, when Rhode Islanders went on board the foundering British revenue schooner Gaspee and burned it to the waterline. At first this generated only regional interest. Then Parliament took up the matter and turned the issue into a public relations disaster for the Crown and a patriot triumph.

Parliament appointed a judicial commission to investigate the ship burning. Many New Englanders quailed with fear when they learned about the commission, for it had authority to send alleged perpetrators to England for trial on treason charges.

Worry about colonists being shipped to London for trial was short-lived. Although a prominent local merchant led those assaulting the ship's crew, Commissioners failed to find any credible witness who would admit knowing any of the culprits' names. Even so, by authorizing the commission and giving it power to send alleged perpetrators of the Gaspee attack to England for trial, the British government generated strong reactions throughout the colonies. The Virginia Gazette copied a Providence Gazette article about the commission and raised questions concerning the commission's constitutional authority to send accused men to England. Picking up on this, in March 1773, the Virginia House of Burgess appointed an eleven-member committee of correspondence to communicate with similar organizations in other colonies, and, indeed, recommended to the other colonial legislatures that they appoint similar committees. These committees were not for show. They engaged in substantive dialogue with their counterparts, and in the process formed a vital link of communication among colonial leaders who, previous to this, had little knowledge of individual patriot leaders outside their own colony.[21]

Legislators in all the mainland colonies recognized the British government's threat to their liberty when it set up a commission to investigate and then send to England anyone accused of participating in an illegal act against the government. Legislators also saw the wisdom in the Virginia Burgesses' recommendation that committees of correspondence maintain contact with counterparts elsewhere. Most of the colonial legislatures had created similar committees by the early fall. New Jersey was the last of the thirteen to join the communications network, on February 8, 1774.[22]

Even before the individual colonial legislatures formulated their committees of correspondence, parliamentary leaders sought a third way of raising revenue while simultaneously confirming their ability to tax colonists. They also saw this new measure as a means of bailing out one of Britain's most venerable and important economic powers. When they did this, they created a challenge of such magnitude that alert patriots saw no option but to respond through direct action against the British government. And that action proved to be a catalyst for dramatic change.

II

Tea Time

In 1773, Parliament passed legislation designed to prevent the East India Company from falling into bankruptcy while simultaneously enticing American colonists to accept Parliament's taxing power over them.

The company and the British Government collaborated on this scheme. Parliament gave the company the extraordinary monopolistic right of shipping tea directly from its London warehouses to specially selected merchant consignees in the colonies. Parliament also agreed to rebate previously charged import taxes on the tea shipped from the East to London, thus making the tea's sale price in the colonies less than Dutch tea smuggled into those same colonies. But in doing so, the government and the company must have realized this arrangement would provoke the ire of merchants who formerly handled tea as an important part of their business, both in England and Scotland, as well as in the colonies. It also chose to ignore the potential the plan created for organized colonial resistance to the sale of taxed tea.[23]

Before exploring these issues, it is time to take a brief look at the East India Company's historic development and then consider its trading and financial situation in the early 1770s.

Near the end of Elizabeth I's reign, at the beginning of the seventeenth century, the monarch granted the predecessor to the

East India Company a fifteen-year monopoly to trade in the East Indies. Called the London East India Company, it was expected to conduct import-export business. The monopoly it enjoyed was to apply only to English ventures, for the obvious reason that the Dutch and the Portuguese already were trading there.

Business activity soon showed that the company would have little success on the export side because English products designed for those living in cool or cold climates were not in demand in the tropics. The company also had challenges at home as critics complained it was shipping out too much specie. And since the company charter had to be renewed from time to time, politics entered the picture.

Following the end of the Cromwellian government, Company leaders became closely attached to the royal Stuart family, in particular James II. When James II was expelled from the country in 1688, Company leaders found themselves on the "outside." When the Dutchman and his English wife, William and Mary, ascended the throne, the company faced an uncertain future. Because William soon found himself needing ready cash, he agreed to issue a second charter for a company trading in the East, and in exchange for a two million pound sterling loan, chartered the English East India Company.

Two competing companies importing goods from India, China, and the East Indies created untenable financial problems for both. Leaders of the two firms began merger negotiations, and in 1709, just a bit over one hundred years after the first company's founding, the original (London) East India Company absorbed its upstart competitor under the formal title of The United Company of Merchants of England Trading in the East Indies—an unwieldy title, quickly shortened in practice to The East India Company.[24]

Half a century later, the East India Company was one of England's largest and most visible business enterprises. In addition to its trading centers in China and elsewhere, it "owned" (administered) important regions of India. For a time, these generated considerable Company profits, which were paid out to

Company stockholders. Its activities in India went well beyond commercial business to include administration and management of the Bengal territory, and periodic military clashes against the French and against Indian armies seeking to retake control of land the company claimed for itself.

A number of East India Company managers and functionaries in India took advantage of the company's fluid, *ad hoc* activities to build personal fortunes. These were difficult for directors in London to ferret out, of course, for communication between London and India took some six months each way, but when these fortune-seekers returned to England, their obvious wealth became an embarrassment to the company, especially when some of the "nabobs"—the derisive term given them—won (or bought) seats in Parliament.

East India Company profits and consequent high dividends to stockholders generated considerable interest among members of Parliament. Some thought the nation should derive benefits from the company beyond the taxes and duties it paid on goods imported to England. With peace restored in 1763, the government turned to the pressing issue of its national debt. The high domestic land tax worried both taxpayers and members of Parliament. Yet the government had to begin repaying its loans. The East India Company, which according to rumors floating across London was generating as much as two million pounds sterling in profit annually from its Bengal property alone, seemed ripe for picking. The rumor most likely stemmed from a letter one of the nabobs sent from India in 1766 to a member of the House of Lords, in which the nabob projected Bengal profits at that level, despite that region's devastating multi-year drought.[25]

Some members of Parliament, including several who were highly placed in the government, owned a substantial number of shares of East India Company stock. Though the prime minister advocated taking government control of the company's territorial claims in India, he was too sick to lead the charge and left the job to others.[26]

The cabinet divided over the issue, and a rather expensive compromise resulted— expensive for the company, that is. Any year the company issued a dividend in excess of 6 percent, it would pay the British government a stipend of 400,000 pounds sterling. The dividend remained well above 6 percent for several succeeding years. But that did not mean the company actually was enjoying substantial profits.[27]

By the early 1770s, Company managers and directors understood business as usual was not working to their benefit, or to that of the stockholders. Turf and control battles within the company, including financial challenges officials in India were generating, frustrated efforts at internal reforms.

Continuing corruption and maladministration, especially among Company agents and representatives in the field, sucked away Company profits. The government helped too by imposing heavy taxes and fees on the import and sale of tea in England, and by this time, tea accounted for as much as half of Company income.

Under British law, all products the company acquired had to be imported to England and duties paid before they could be exported to any of Britain's colonies. While the resulting high price for tea might limit the number of purchasers in Britain or the colonies, the company still should have had a reasonably good sales volume. Unfortunately for the company, Britain's customs service at home and in the colonies was not well equipped to counter smuggling. As a result, by the late 1760s, English and Scottish merchants were smuggling in an amazing amount of tea—over seven million pounds of Dutch tea annually—and selling it at prices well below what the East India Company could offer for its tea, since the Dutch did not tax tea imported to its country for subsequent export.[28]

Smuggling activities in the American colonies did not rise to a significant level until 1768, when the colonists began boycotting all British goods in opposition to the Townshend revenue duties. Creative merchants in New York and Philadelphia, and to a lesser extent in smaller ports, soon had reasonably safe routes worked out for smuggling Dutch tea into their colonies. This came by way of either the Netherlands or its West Indies outpost. Though the quality of Dutch Bohea tea was inferior to Bohea tea brought in from England, it served the needs and wants of voracious American tea sippers. For the two years of the boycott, many American colonists lived off the smuggled Dutch tea.[29]

When the boycott ended with Parliament repealing all the Townshend Duties except the tea tax, merchants who had well-established smuggling routes saw no reason to abandon them, especially since popular opposition to paying a tax to Britain remained high in the middle colonies. Only in New England and the South did purchases of East India Company tea return to levels close to those the company had enjoyed in the mid-1760s. In fact in 1771 and '72, Company exports to the thirteen American colonies were less than half what they had been five years earlier. Observers on both sides of the Atlantic who kept track of the tea industry estimated that after the colonists ended their boycott of British goods in 1770, approximately nine of ten pounds of tea purchased in the colonies was Dutch rather than English. Yet this problem was really just an unpleasant aggravation to the tea situation in Britain.[30]

High import taxes combined with inland duties on tea sold within Britain virtually doubled the price at retail outlets. This made smuggled tea a valuable commodity for merchants because it meant larger than usual profits. The company provided Parliament with enough evidence of this problem that a law enacted in 1767 lowered the total tax on tea for a five-year period. Sales of East India Company tea soared. Sales volume soon surpassed 6.5 million pounds annually. Though this accounted for less than half the tea sold in Britain, it provided a significant increase in Company profits.

The reduced tea tax had a statutory limit of five years. When taxes returned to their previous levels in 1772, Company sales dropped accordingly so that annual sales within Britain fell to some four million pounds, a drop of 38 percent. Yet Company tea imports remained high. Further heightening the problem was a collapse of the financial markets in England. This led to a major recession across the land and, indeed, well into Europe.[31]

Company tea, whether for domestic consumption or for export, was sold through semiannual auctions held in London. Spring sales in 1772 proved disappointing, but after the recession severely slowed commercial activities, the fall 1772 sale was an utter failure. Because of this, Company warehouses were groaning under the weight of tea: some seventeen million pounds of tea. That was bad enough, but Company finances posed a worse—and immediate—problem.

Routinely, the East India Company requested and secured a loan from the Bank of England to cover its expenses before it received payments from its semiannual auctions in London. In 1772, the loan had been for 300,000 pounds sterling. When the fall auction failed, the company asked the bank for an extension. Given the financial crises swirling around London at the time, the bank refused to grant the extension. Then there was the debt to the government. The company owed at least one million pounds sterling in taxes and duties on its imports. Yet the company had little in the way of cash reserves, and certainly not nearly enough to cover its debts.

An immediate, perplexing problem.

Powerful Company directors were haughty men projecting high egos, but they could not ignore the company's financial distress. Early in 1773, the company petitioned the Government for a 1.5 million pound sterling loan. Accompanying that request was a pledge to reform the Bengal territory administration.[32]

Of course, the company's financial difficulties were well known across London, and Lord North's administration had, in fact, convened Parliament in a special session to consider both that matter and the government's relations with the company. The company and the Bank of England formed the cornerstone of Britain's economy. Clearly, the East India Company was too important for the government to allow it to fail.

Two parliamentary committees were conducting investigations, but eventually Prime Minister North took charge of restructuring not only the company debt but also the company's internal administration as well as that of its territories in India. The self-assured determination with which the administration acted, and the magnitude of those actions against a chartered corporation of more than a century and a half's standing surprised many, angered some, struck fear in others, but made clear to all that the North administration would advance its own agenda. Indeed, one of Lord North's principal opponents in the House of Lords wrote to a trusted friend in October 1772:

> All thinking men must already acknowledge that the influence of the Crown and the means of corruption are become very dangerous to the Constitution and yet the enormous addition of power which Government are aiming at by subjecting the East India Company to their control does not strike and alarm as much as it ought.[33]

The North administration's plan included a loan to the company of 1.4 million pounds sterling; restrictions on the company's dividends, limiting them to 6 percent per year until the loan was repaid; a requirement that the company split its profits with the government; the assumption that the government eventually would take control of Bengal and adjacent areas in India, and in the interim, the government would appoint Bengal's Governor General and his advisory council members. Lord North also proposed to restrict voting rights of shareholders who chose members of the company's General Court by doubling the minimum value of stock required to cast a vote.[34]

There was no question the government's plan altered the company's royal charter, which the monarch, not Parliament, had authorized, or that it intended to appropriate for itself Company property by act of Parliament, rather than through judicial proceedings. Despite members of the parliamentary opposition's agonized cries of foul and charges of tyranny leveled against Lord

North, there also was no question that the North administration had the votes to pass its Regulating Act.

Company directors considered their situation, and, in desperation, sought to withdraw the loan request. Lord North responded by writing into the Regulating Act a requirement that the company take the loan.

Ultimately, Prime Minister North eased some of the harshest financial penalties inflicted on the company but kept in place requirements that the company reform its administration, keeping Government power to appoint the manager of Bengal, and plans to assume eventual control of that territory. In the process, though, the government accepted the company's new suggestions that it receive special treatment for tea exported to the American colonies.[35]

Aware that the company was awash with tea, one of its correspondents suggested petitioning the government for a refund of import duties on tea exported, and then developing a market for it in Europe. Company officials communicated with several persons knowledgeable in the European trade and received discouraging responses. Not only was that market more variable than they had been led to believe but because the European ports were so close to England, smugglers were likely to purchase un-dutied tea shipped there and then return it to the mother country, further reducing the company's domestic market. That led to a bright idea.[36]

Why not petition for a rebate of duties on tea that was exported and ship it to America? To improve profit potential, why not get government approval to ship the tea to select merchants in America's largest cities, thus eliminating middleman costs? Further, the company could do this without fear of the tea being smuggled back to England, since the shipping costs would be too great for such a scheme to generate a profit. In working through these ideas, the directors also considered favorably the idea of proposing that the three pence [penny] per pound duty on tea shipped into America be dropped. This would almost assuredly mean Company tea would undersell smuggled Dutch tea.

The company drew up an amendment to its petition to Parliament and sent it to Lord North. It proposed having the government refund taxes paid on imported tea which was then exported to America and providing authority for the company to ship the tea directly to merchant consignees in America. Somehow in the process of drawing up this petition, Company directors omitted the request that the Townshend tea tax be dropped.[37]

Lord North approved the proposals and incorporated them into what became known as the Tea Act. Debate then resumed in Parliament, where members focused primarily on the Regulating Act. After all, the special session into which members of Parliament had been called was designed to see that the East India Company was given a financial transfusion while also being reformed. One aspect of returning the company to financial solvency was to facilitate its sale of tea in the colonies.

While most members of Parliament concerned themselves with financing and reorganizing the East India Company, some gave close attention to the bill authorizing the company to ship tea directly to American colonies. They raised the question of the Townshend tea tax. Was it also to be rescinded? Indeed, a veteran member of Parliament made a fateful prediction. "I tell the Noble Lord now, if he don't take off the duty they [the colonists] won't take the tea."[38]

Lord North responded that he had considered the matter and decided to retain the tax for "political reasons." Some two years later, Lord North offered a weak defense of his decision to retain the tax. His remarks were summarized in Cobbett's Parliamentary History:

> It was impossible for him [Lord North] to have foreseen the proceedings in America respecting the tea; that the duty had been quietly collected before; that the great quantity of tea in the warehouses of the East India Company...made it necessary to do something for the benefit of the company... that it was impossible for him to foretell the Americans would resist being able to drink their tea...cheaper.[39]

A member of Parliament who also sat on the East India Company Court of Directors kept the prime minister's feet to the fire. He noted that representatives of the company had talked with Lord North about dropping the Townshend tea tax. He said that he had "intreated" with Lord North to remove the tax and "fortold the consequence of persevering in error...." He added: "I protested against it, as contrary to the principles of their monopoly. Yet the power of the ministry prevailed." This gives credence to the argument that Lord North had, as King George III urged, retained the tea tax on the colonies as a means of proving Parliament's supremacy over those colonies.[40]

With Parliament's agreement to rebate the import duty on tea, and its authority for the East India Company to ship tea directly from its warehouses to merchant consignees in America, plans went ahead in the summer of 1773 to unload part of the company's surplus tea on the colonies. London merchants doing business with counterparts in the colonies, along with several colonial merchants who were in the city, inundated the company with recommendations for merchants in Boston, New York, Philadelphia, and Charleston to serve as Company agents in those cities.[41]

Even so, all did not go smoothly, for a number of American ship captains, including one who captained a vessel John Hancock owned, refused to accept consignments from the company for delivery in the colonies. In addition, officials of the East India Company received warnings from American merchants that shipping duted tea to America might provoke negative reactions because of popular sentiment in opposition to the Townshend tea duty. Gilbert Barkly, a Philadelphia merchant, warned the company that:

> The duty of 3d. [penny] per lb. some time ago laid on teas payable in America, gave the colonials great umbrage, and occasioned their smuggling that article into the country...

which, from the extent of the coast…cannot be prevented by custom officers, or the king's cruizers, and as the wisdom of Parliament recons it impolitical to take off this duty, the colonials will persevere in purchasing that article in the usual manner [of smuggling]. …

In a separate letter he proposed: "The company being the exporters, pays the American duty of 3d. per lb., of which they will be amply repaid by the advance of their sales. …" Under this arrangement, Barkly seemed to hope the colonists might think they were not paying an illegal tax, and proceed to purchase English tea. (In hindsight, there is little reason to believe this hope would have been fulfilled.)

Another correspondent with the company pointed out that the company annually sold some 600,000 pounds sterling of cloth from India to the colonies, and the plan to sell taxed tea in large quantities would endanger future cloth sales because "it might defeat the one and prejudice the other."

Had the company offered small consignments to each targeted American port, their investment in a plan they knew was fraught with danger would have been minimized. But no, they put nearly 600,000 pounds of tea at risk, and incurred a devastating loss.[42]

Benjamin Franklin's work in London had kept him away from the colonies for several years, but he was well informed on changing sentiments there and indicated his belief that the tea shipments would not be well received. He wrote to the Massachusetts Speaker of the lower house, one of the colony's most influential political leaders, in June 1773:

> …the scheme is, to take off as much duty as will make the tea cheaper in America than foreigners can supply us, and continue the duty there to keep up the exercise of the right. They have no idea that any people can act from any principle but that of interest; and they believe that 3d. in a pound of tea…is sufficient to overcome all the patriotism of an American.[43]

Apparently only after sending out seven ships laden with tea to the colonies did some in the East India Company began to worry about its fate. In fact, this concern may have arisen when Lord Dartmouth, Secretary for America, met with the company chairman. Ironically, their meeting occurred less than a week after the Boston Tea Party was held. Even though it now was too late to take corrective action, Company officials sought information from local merchants doing business with counterparts in Boston, New York, Philadelphia, and Charleston, asking whether they had received word on the possible fate of the tea shipments. The responses were qualified at best. A Boston merchant had noted in an October letter that "if one is to credit the [newspaper] prints, no small opposition will be made thereto. However I am in hopes it will be otherwise. ..." A New York merchant wrote the first week of November that "The introduction of the East India Company's tea is violently opposed here, by a set of men who shamefully live by monopolizing tea in the smuggling way." But another New Yorker sent a letter the same week in which he warned that if the three pence duty was attached to the tea's sale, "I am much in doubt whether it will be safe, as almost every body in that case speaks against the admission of it. ..." A London merchant whose brother was his correspondent in Philadelphia told the company that "it was very doubtful how [the tea] would be received there, the measure being looked upon in an unfavorable view in general." Another Philadelphian said, "I do not believe one man in a hundred was to be met who approved of the sending of the tea, while the duty was to be paid here." The London correspondents with South Carolina reported receiving no information from there. But with essentially negative responses from three of four colonial ports, East India Company officials must have faced a bleak Christmas season.[44]

While having Parliament pass legislation intended to save one of Britain's most powerful companies from financial ruin, Lord

North instigated Company action that led to the loss of perhaps half of Britain's first empire.

Before considering American patriots' reaction to Parliament's Tea Act, we will survey a transformative period in colonial history when many people, but especially thousands of working class colonists, gained a new perspective on their lives. Looking briefly at this remarkable intellectual, spiritual, and emotional earthquake is important because the people, or in some cases the children of the people, who transformed themselves in the process were largely responsible for the revolution.

III

A Spiritual Awakening
of the Heart Prepared Colonists
to Oppose British Tyranny

When a farmer takes on the task of creating a new field, he first clears it of rocks and stumps, in preparation for plowing and then planting seeds for a crop.

In the case we are considering, evangelists cleared individuals' hearts of spiritual rocks and stumps, and prepared them to receive seeds of redemption.

Jonathan Edwards might have been a humble minister in a small New England town, but his heart and his brain were as large as the continent. In the following passage he explained how he was able to begin a vital spiritual transformation among members of his congregation:

> God has also seemed to have gone out of his usual way in the quickness of his work, and the swift progress his Spirit has made in his operations on the hearts of many. 'Tis wonderful that persons should be so suddenly, and yet so greatly, changed: many have been taken from a loose and careless way of living, and seized with strong convictions of

their guilt and misery, and in a very little time "old things have passed away, and all things have become new with them."

So wrote The Reverend Jonathan Edwards in an essay on the religious revival he led in Northampton, Massachusetts during 1734 and 1735.[45]

The Northampton revival was the prelude to what those at the time referred to as "The Great Awakening," and what most historians today refer to as the First Great Awakening. Though several earlier revivals were recorded elsewhere in previous decades, the widespread excitement (and in some places resentment or criticism) this revival generated, coupled with the towering intellectual power Jonathan Edwards projected for the ensuing twenty years give Northampton as the location, and Edwards as the human motivating force for this religious Awakening.

But why raise here the subject of a religious revival in the 1730s and '40s?

The short answer is this revival and its continuing after-effects fundamentally changed hundreds of thousands of middle class colonials' outlook and self-assuredness. Beginning in New England, moving into the middle colonies, and reaching the southern colonies through their frontier regions, the Great Awakening's spiritual and moral messages, as well as the character-building activities which followed, changed the outlook "the middling sort" or "the lower orders" of colonists brought to their interaction with each other as well as with their "betters." These experiences caused many of them to give new value to their lives, to their relations with their neighbors and fellow townspeople—young and old, rich and poor—and to their involvement in public affairs.

From 1765 on, rising American protests against Parliament's attempts to restrict the workings of colonial governments, and Parliament's assault on colonists' liberties, could hardly have been effective without cooperation among the economic and social elite, and middle and lower class citizens.

Starting in the seventeenth century, when England chartered North American colonies, once a newly planted settlement survived the "starving time" and emerged with a viable economy and a responsible government, "deference" became the mode of social and political intercourse. This was, however elementary the colonial development might have been, a kind of replication of English society.

A colony elite formed itself and assumed control over major economic and governmental institutions. In the case of the latter, while colonies held elections for legislative representatives, where virtually all property owners could participate, usually only the prosperous stood for office. Yes, they might curry favor with small landholders, retailers, and master craftsmen who comprised the majority of eligible voters, but those middling sort generally would not challenge them in an election.

In social intercourse, farmers, storekeepers, small merchants, and skilled artisans who had a comfortable living protected their economic interests by showing appropriate deference to the affluent. On Sunday, while all economic classes might participate in the same worship service, the elite often had pews reserved for them. In some churches the affluent purchased pew rights. Even in an academic setting, some colleges ranked students not by achievement, but by social/economic class.

Following the French and Indian War, tensions between colonies and mother country rose. As we have seen, American patriots organized protest groups that provided both leadership and manpower to put potent economic boycotts into effect. Especially in cities and towns, these organizations of necessity relied on members of the middle class for boycott enforcement activities, but almost all of these patriotic organizations included prominent and wealthy citizens on their rolls.

As parliamentary action stimulated the patriots to consider military preparation, volunteer militias organized themselves. Usually, the rank and file troops elected their officers. While "deference" continued to play its part in the economic and social life of communities, increasingly members of "the middling sort" exerted independent judgment, and many chose to seek—and claim—leadership positions.

Several factors may have influenced actions members of the middle class chose to take in local or colony-wide organizations. But one of the most significant factors was their development of a coherent religious outlook. That development began to show itself in New England in the 1740s. It expanded geographically from north to south over the following three decades, paving the way for extensive cooperation among patriots of all economic levels. They banded together to resist British aggression and defend, first the colonies and then the new American nation.

This is not to imply that all who participated actively in these revivals became ardent patriots. Indeed, some chose to be equally passionate supporters of the king and Parliament. The point here is that the religious experiences gave many middle-class men and women a new, positive perspective on their own worth.

While there is no consensus among historians as to the Awakening's beginning and duration, New Englanders certainly led the way. Puritanism, as practiced with great dedication and intellectual strength in Massachusetts Bay in the 1630s, gradually declined in spirit and vigor, so that by the last third of the seventeenth century clergy in many churches preached a sterile, dry, abstract theology. Instead of helping members seek divine inspiration or find a divine avenue to salvation, ministers focused on esoteric interpretations of biblical scripture.

Near the end of the seventeenth century a few clergymen reinvigorated their messages and urged parishioners to give serious consideration to their relationship with God. They were an exception that failed to catch the attention of other clergy or the church laity. Then, in the early 1720s, a genuine revival erupted in the Connecticut River Valley, but the enthusiasm generated there did not carry over into neighboring colonies, and even that local enthusiasm dissipated.

In 1734, Jonathan Edwards, later recognized as the most powerful theologian of the eighteenth century, initiated a major revival in his church in Northampton, Massachusetts. At first focusing on the youth who were suffering the shock of a friend's death, he expanded his preaching to the entire congregation. Before long, he was speaking in other churches as well.

The Reverend Edwards's message was that there was only one avenue to divine grace. In a sermon which was, in essence, the keystone of his preaching, he said "it is none of our own excellency, virtue, or righteousness, that is the ground of our being received from a state of condemnation into a state of acceptance in God's sight, but only Jesus Christ, and his righteousness, and worthiness, received by faith."[46]

Edwards based his argument about "justification by faith" on the Bible's Book of Romans, Chapters 9 and 10, which reads, in part:

> What shall we say then? That the Gentiles, who did not pursue righteousness, have attained it, that is righteousness by faith; but that Israel, who pursued a law that would lead to righteousness, did not succeed in reaching that law. Why? Because they did not pursue it by faith, but as if it were based on works. They have stumbled over the stumbling stone, as it is written, Behold, I am laying in Zion a stone of stumbling, and a rock of offence: and whosoever believeth in him will not be put to shame. ... For Christ is the end of the law for righteousness to everyone who believes. ... For with the heart one believes and is justified, and with the mouth one confesses and is saved. For the Scripture says, "Everyone who believes in him will not be put the shame." For there is no distinction between Jew and Greek.... For "everyone who calls on the name of the Lord will be saved."[47]

Edwards's message: that one must "believe in thine heart" in order to achieve salvation, resonated with men and women who had a practical bent toward life. Many of them had not been stirred by the intellectual sermons of Congregational or Episcopal (Anglican) divines who had learned their theology as students in religiously conservative colleges. But the messages Edwards preached were stirring, often generating emotional outpourings among congregation members.

Edwards tried to discourage spontaneous outcries during his sermons, for he feared they would distract his listeners. He hoped to keep their attention on his message and thus promote both Bible study and personal reflection in the days following the sermon.

While Edwards stimulated laypersons and clergy alike to undertake renewed study of and inquiry into the Christian message, a British Anglican minister's itinerant preachings—those of George Whitefield—soon eclipsed Edwards's influence.

Whitefield attended Oxford University, where, in 1735, he was converted to Christian spirituality. Soon after, he began his evangelical preaching career. He preached in both England and Wales, where he often drew throngs of followers, too many for a church. When this situation arose, Whitefield preached in adjacent fields. Then, undertaking a mission to the colonies in 1739, he conducted an extensive preaching trip up the Atlantic coast. While his preaching stirred the hearts and minds of many, Whitefield actually used new techniques to draw large crowds. He saw that his schedule was published well ahead in local newspapers, and he readily spoke with journalists about his work, thus bringing what today would be called public relations techniques into play. Beyond that, on a more substantive level, Whitefield met with both Anglican and dissenting ministers to discuss their work and explain his. This appears to be the first time an ordained Anglican priest worked openly and cooperatively with dissenting ministers. While the results were not always happy, Whitefield was making the point that the minister's first priority was that of promoting the individual's "new birth" rather than preserving denominational purity. Indeed, these encounters, whether positive or negative, set the tone for evangelical initiatives that were to take place over the coming decades.[48]

Often preaching to several thousand avid listeners, Whitefield's messages prompted many churchgoers to question their regular minister's biblical interpretations. One aftermath of his preaching in some communities was a congregational split over theological issues. Such splits sometimes resulted in breakaway congregations simply creating new churches of the same denomination. In other cases, the departing members organized a church and either became independent or attached it to a different denomination. The most frequent of the latter were to the Baptist denomination.

Before 1740, Baptist congregations in New England numbered fewer than ten. As the Awakening movement impacted that region, desertions from established Congregational churches, coupled with the creations of new towns by floods of immigrants into the northern parts of the region, generated many new Baptist churches. By the end of the century, New England had over three hundred Baptist congregations. No doubt, most of these were formed in the 1740s, '50s, and '60s.[49]

This dramatic change was not solely due to Whitefield's preaching. A number of young clergymen followed in his footsteps and preached with great enthusiasm. Beyond this, many laypersons became itinerant preachers, especially in frontier regions. In the middle colonies evangelical preachers enjoyed a ready-made audience among the thousands of recently arrived Scotch-Irish immigrants to Pennsylvania and the Jerseys.

Itinerant ministers also worked their way into the South, especially the piedmont (interior, or western) areas of Virginia and the Carolinas. Government officials responsible for maintaining the established Anglican Church in Virginia sometimes challenged them, but local converts managed to keep the dissenting church assemblies going. In fact, between the end of the 1760s and the start of the Revolution, Baptist churches in Virginia increased from seven to over fifty.

Despite having to pay taxes in support of the local Anglican Church, Virginia dissenters also financed their own church. But sometimes they faced even more severe hardships. In 1771, a Baptist congregation was meeting when the local Anglican minister, accompanied by his clerk, the sheriff, and some others interrupted the service. The preacher of the Baptist group, Brother Waller, began praying, when:

> he was Violently Jerked off of the Stage, [they] Caught him by the Back part of his Neck[,] Beat his head against the ground, some Times Up[,] Sometimes down, they Carried him through the Gate that stood some Considerable Distance, where a Gentleman [the sheriff] Give him ... Twenty Lashes with his Horse Whip. ... Then B[rother] Waller was Released, Went Back Singing praises to God, Mounted the Stage & preached with a Great Deal of Liberty.

When asked about the pain and suffering he endured, Brother Walker "answer'd that the Lord stood by him...& pour'd his Love into his Soul without measure, & the Bretheren and Sisters Round him Singing praises...so that he Could Scarcely feel the stripes...."

Walker had continued the service, "Rejoicing...that he was Worthy to Suffer for his Dear Lord & Master."[50]

This willingness of Baptists and others to persevere in publicly practicing their faith despite such brutal persecution indicates the strength of character such people developed, whether they suffered physical pain directly or were witnesses to it. Yet remarkably, four years later, many of these same dissenters freely joined with Virginia planter elites (who almost invariably were Anglican parishioners) in opposing British aggression.

As Colin Bonwick, a British historian, has noted, these dissenting Virginia colonists "did not challenge order as such, quite the reverse, but offered an alternative model to traditional prescriptive hierarchy; their ultimate authority was not secular but that of God discovered by personal experience."[51]

In New England and New York, where colonies had "established" (government supported) churches, despite important doctrinal differences, dissenting clergy gradually learned to work together to protect each other and their flocks of parishioners. Part of their shared endeavor involved promoting the idea of religious liberty. They were especially active in opposing the appointment of an Anglican Bishop for the colonies, fearing such an appointment would be followed with the imposition of ecclesiastical courts that could threaten their very existence.

Colonists criticized the establishment of the Catholic Church in Quebec after Britain gained control of Canada. This was not just a matter of religious intolerance. It was a fear that established churches anywhere in the empire would impinge on their religious liberty. Most of those who opposed the idea of an established Catholic Church in Canada (and down into the Ohio Valley) also opposed with equal vigor the widespread establishment of the Anglican Church in the colonies, from which the appointment of a Bishop might follow.

The growing advocacy of religious freedom gave individuals an increased appreciation and support for cooperation among denominational and independent congregations, locally, colony-wide, and among neighboring colonies. This attitude carried over to the economic and political battles that emerged following the French and Indian War.

But, back to the Great Awakening. While this movement generated controversy and division among existing congregations— often heated, bitter conflict—and stimulated formation of new church assemblies, its moving force was directed at an individual's reform and salvation. And that emphasis generated important stimuli for people of all economic classes to participate in protests and later military conflict with the British.

Simply saying that the Awakening changed individual lives gives no impression of its power. Here are two examples taken from writings of plain people who wanted to leave a record of their experiences.

Nathan Cole, a Connecticut farmer, wrote of his encounter with George Whitefield when the latter preached in Middletown, Connecticut, in 1740. Cole then described the eventual consequence of that encounter.

Cole began his narrative by announcing: "I was born Feb 15, 1711, and born again octo [October] 1741." He continued, saying as a young man he believed he could obtain salvation "by my own works such as prayers and good deeds." Then he heard about Whitefield's preaching and "longed to see and hear him preach the Gospel."

Someone told Cole that Whitefield would be preaching in Middletown later that morning. "I dropt the tool I had in my hand and ran home to my wife telling her to make ready quickly to go." The two of them rode to Middletown on his workhorse. As they neared the town they saw a cloud of dust, which soon turned out to be caused by hundreds of others pursuing the same goal they were. He was told the crowd numbered up to four thousand people. Even so, he was able to see and hear Whitefield when the evangelist spoke. Cole was almost physically struck by Whitefield's message: "My hearing him preach, gave me a heart wound; By God's blessing my old Foundation was broken up, and I saw that my righteousness would not save me; then I was convinced of the doctrine of Election and went right to quarrelling with God about it...."

Cole left Middletown and returned to his farm feeling distraught. Though Whitefield's message had had an intense emotional impact on the man, Cole believed in his heart he had not received God's blessing. In subsequent months he suffered great anxiety, for he was convinced God had not blessed him.

Eventually, fear turned to joy. "When God appeared to me every thing vanished and was gone in the twinkling of an Eye, as quick as A flash of lightening; But when God disappeared or in some measure withdrew, every thing was in its place again and I was on my Bed. ..." Cole then assessed his experience: "I was set free, my distress was gone, and I was filled with a pineing desire to see Christs own words in the bible. ...." He continued describing his extended reaction to his experience with God, concluding: "now my heart and Soul were filled as full as they Could hold with Joy and sorrow; now I perfectly felt truth: now my heart talked with God...."[52]

In 1742, an unnamed illiterate man described his recent experience to someone who wrote it and kept it for posterity. "On Tuesday last I being at a meeting Mr. Pomeroy preached.... I found my heart in some measure drawn forth to God." When the service was concluded, "my soul was filled with ravishing transport to that degree it seemed there was nothing but a thin paper wall that separated me from perfect glory."

The narrator described how a dove transported him over an imposing mountain. He then passed a roaring bull. Next, an angel led him to "a place I thought was heaven. ...." At last, "I thought I saw God the Father and God the Son seated on a throne of glory. ...." He said Christ spoke to him, but he could not answer. Amazingly, he was shown a book with his name written in blood, and was told he would eventually return, but for now he must go home. On the way home, with the dove's aid, he witnessed a terrifying sight. "I saw the mouth of hell open and the damned souls wallowing in the flames...." When the devil threatened him, "I heard a voice: 'Fear thou not, I am with thee; be not dismayed, I am thy God.'" He said Satan disappeared into the flames. "Then my senses returned to me...."[53]

These two religious conversion descriptions illustrate the intense experiences thousands of individuals reported in the 1740s, '50s, and '60s (and, indeed, on into the nineteenth century, when a "Second Great Awakening" transpired). Those experiences caused many persons to develop a different, more confident outlook on life. If God said they were worthy human beings, deserving to live on into eternity, then surely they had more to contribute to their neighbors and the community than they previously had thought.

As individuals and families broke away from one church and founded a new congregation, those actively involved in the process gained new confidence. Many of these were working people. Amazingly, they found themselves taking greater individual responsibility for the life of those in the congregation than had been the case in the staid, established churches. Such involvement also gave individuals opportunities to develop the capacity to express themselves clearly, to organize special projects and programs, and to become leaders.

Of course, while many were "born again" during those decades, others maintained their established religious concepts and traditional relations with their ministers and fellow parishioners. Some well-regarded ministers even ridiculed the young upstarts. In "A Discourse on Christian Union," published in Boston in 1760, the Reverend Ezra Stiles commented about the Awakening: "Multitudes were seriously, soberly and solemnly out of their wits."[54]

But, more recent assessments of the religious upheaval include:

> Out of the Awakening came new ideas—the many propositions that "American society, having been shaken by the experience, was henceforth consciously to observe." The Great Awakening thus stands as a major example of that most elusive of phenomena: a turning point, a "crisis," in the history of American civilization.

And another observation is that in Virginia, "the Great Awakening [w]as a crisis of authority that prepared the way for the Revolution among both the colonial elite and lower orders." [55]

After gaining their spiritual independence, many individuals were equipped to consider their political dependence on a distant nation that seemed determined to push them into a servant class rather than allowing them liberty of action. Indeed, many colonists looked at parliamentary policies and reconsidered their formerly competitive attitudes toward their Atlantic neighbors. One historian has noted: "After 1763, British policy drastically changed the context of colonial politics. It encouraged incipient

American nationalism and propelled the colonies towards a voluntary union."[56]

The rising tide of mid-century religious ferment provided colonists with a growing sense of intellectual maturity. This generated added headaches for parliamentary leaders. After the close of the French and Indian War, parliamentary leaders sought to impose new restrictions on colonists and make what the colonists considered unconstitutional financial demands. Colonists countered these intrusions into their life and government through political theory and economic force. As we will see in the next chapter, some of the colonists' "new" political theories were, in fact, taken from doctrines developed during the "Glorious Revolution" of 1688-89, when King James II was chased from the throne. Just as Jonathan Edwards, George Whitefield, and their successors gave fresh, new interpretations to long-familiar Biblical passages, so politically astute colonists brought fresh, dynamic interpretations to old, formally proclaimed doctrines, and in doing so ignited the interest and garnered the support of thousands of fellow colonists.

IV
Political Ideas:
Some Fresh, Others Stale

Slow as cross-ocean ships were in the eighteenth century, with travel each way normally taking four to six weeks, the flow of information and ideas did not stop at the water's edge. "News" of events a month old was still "new" to those who received it.

In America, colonists' thirst for news, stories of happenings within their own colony, information on events in other American colonies, and reports from England, grew steadily in the 1760s and 1770s. This is evidenced by the increase in the number and circulation of newspapers. In 1763, at the end of the French and Indian War, twenty-three newspapers were being published. Twelve years later, when Americans were deciding whether to declare their independence from Britain, thirty-eight papers were in circulation. There was at least one in every colony except Delaware, which had no substantial urban center. It relied on those printed in nearby Philadelphia.[57]

With no hindrance of copyright to restrain them, editors freely copied each other's news reports or essays. Packet ships brought London newspapers to the ports, and colonial editors selected excerpts or whole stories for republication in their upcoming editions. The reverse held as well. British newspaper editors avidly read American publications and copied those stories or essays they thought would help them sell newspapers in London or elsewhere.

One continuing story which captured the imagination on both sides of the Atlantic, and stoked American patriots' fear of British political tyranny, had to do with a running fight between a rakish British commoner and sometime member of the House of Commons and the king, his ministers, and the courts of law. That story, radically shortened into a slogan, served to symbolize American passion for preserving "liberty" in the face of growing British oppression.

When the diplomats signed the Peace of Paris of 1763, Britain's costliest war ended. Simultaneously, France's power in North America evaporated. Yet not everyone in London was happy.

John Wilkes, in fact, was furious at young King George III (aged twenty-five and only in his third year as monarch) for forcing what he considered a hasty and unwise peace settlement. Fanning that anger was the fact that the treaty had been negotiated under the man the king had chosen to replace the nation's war leader (a popular hero) as prime minister. And that new man, Lord Bute (a name critical crowds changed to "Boot"), was a detested Scotchman! In fact, polemicists ignited the flames of hatred toward Bute, causing him to surround himself with bodyguards when he went to Parliament. Not surprisingly, he resigned his post shortly after both sides signed the treaty.[58]

Wilkes, with the aid of his mentor, Lord Temple, had gone into the publishing business, printing The North Briton. It was designed almost solely to attack the government directly and the king indirectly. But when the king came to prorogue (close) Parliament in April 1763, and in his speech praised the peace treaty, Wilkes ridiculed George III's statement in The North Briton's issue Number 45.[59]

Highly incensed, the king sought retribution. He ordered Wilkes arrested on a charge of libel. The question was, though, whether a member of the House of Commons—of which Wilkes was one—could be arrested for libel. The attorney general claimed that privileges members of the Commons enjoyed did not extend to protection against a libel charge.

One of the Secretaries of State had a general search warrant issued to find and collect evidence in regard to the case. A general search warrant was equivalent to "a fishing expedition," naming no person and no documents. Furthermore, it was not limited to searching a specific building. This general search warrant was issued without any evidence in hand regarding Wilkes's role in writing or publishing the offending document.

After a series of fumbles and miscues, government agents took Wilkes to be interviewed; then he was confined to the Tower of London. Other government agents searched Wilkes's home with a heavy hand and also arrested forty-nine individuals, including ordinary printers and typesetters.[60]

In relatively short order, Lord Temple went to a judge who neither the king nor the prime minister controlled and secured a writ of Habeas Corpus, freeing Wilkes. In subsequent court judgments, general search warrants were deemed unconstitutional, and a verdict rendered that members of Parliament were exempt from prosecution on a charge of libel.[61]

Members of the Commons conducted a furious, intemperate debate over the Wilkes matter. Realizing he might be vulnerable to further action, Wilkes fled to France. The Commons, which the prime minister controlled, expelled him from membership.

Wilkes was a free man while in France, but King George III was a stubborn individual, and he had the forces and resources of government behind him. The king's ministers filed new charges against Wilkes. When Wilkes remained in France rather than face the charges, the court declared him an outlaw.

Instead of silencing Wilkes and smothering the story, the king's ministers' actions built a massive following on Wilkes's behalf, both in England and America. The man became a symbol for British (and American) rights: freedom of the press; a man's home is his castle and cannot be invaded without just cause; citizens have a right to be represented in Parliament (or in a colonial legislature) by whomever they choose. By the mid-1760s, "Wilkes and Liberty" toasts were commonplace in American taverns. Signs appeared, and clothing was bedecked with "45," representing the offending North Briton issue. Yet the story did not end there.[62]

Returning to London in 1768, Wilkes announced his candidacy for a seat in the House of Commons and promised to submit to a court hearing after the election. With massive popular support, he was elected. His conviction on a four-year-old charge followed, and he again went to prison.

Reasoning that Wilkes's confinement would end when Parliament reconvened, a massive crowd gathered in St. George's Fields to celebrate "Wilkes and Liberty." Then news arrived that Wilkes would not be released. The crowd became raucous. Local magistrates called out the troops to quell the mob. Soldiers killed or wounded several people, including a boy who was chased into a house and deliberately shot. In short order, the soldier involved in killing the boy was charged with murder, then tried and acquitted.[63]

Newspapers in America soon reported the boy's death and wrote of the troops killing other Londoners. Bostonians drew a parallel to the boy's death when, in February 1770, a person in Boston thought to be a government informer murdered an eleven-year-old boy.[64]

A short time later the St. George's Field killings became significant in America when, on March 5, 1770, British troops fired into a hostile crowd, killing five, and creating the "Boston Massacre." The parallel stories of armed aggression on unarmed civilians were an obvious opportunity for local patriots. At least that was how colonial Whig (meaning patriot) newspapers pictured them. Fear of the British government sending in a standing army to stifle dissent grew in America and appeared to be a reality in Boston. A distinguished member of the Massachusetts Governor's Council wrote an emotional description of the "Massacre" which was published in pamphlet form and distributed throughout the colonies. Claiming that the armed assault in the center of Boston had been deliberate, the pamphleteer drew parallels with the St.

George's Field killings. He also paralleled the acquittal of the accused troops in both cases, leaving open questions as to how those acquittals had been accomplished. He left no question, though, that both assaults resulted from cynical governmental motivation to intimidate the populace.[65]

Back in London, Parliament refused to accept the duly elected Wilkes and declared his seat vacant. The electorate returned Wilkes to the Commons seat unanimously twice more, with the House each time immediately denying him his seat. Finally, the prime minister found an opponent to challenge Wilkes. In the election Wilkes garnered over 1,100 votes; his opponent fewer than 300. Yet, again, the prime minister forced the Commons to reject Wilkes and arranged his opponent's seating.[66]

In the American colonies, newspapers reported every aspect of the Wilkes case. For a government to reject so blatantly "the will of the people" generated increasing speculation about that government's intentions with respect to controlling—possibly dominating—American life.

Colonists wrote to Wilkes offering support. After his followers in England created a Society of the Supporters of the Bill of Rights, individual colonists sent donations across the Atlantic to help fill the Society's coffers.[67]

In December 1769, the South Carolina Lower House voted a 1,500-pound sterling donation from the colony's common fund to the Society. The governor informed his superiors in London about the donation. Angered that the South Carolina lower house was supporting the British government's most vocal critic, the Attorney General stated that the manner in which the Lower House had appropriated funds was unconstitutional, though it conformed with a practice which had been in existence for some forty years.

The attorney general's opinion generated a new conflict between the South Carolina Lower House and the governor and his council, which had to enforce the British attorney general's decision. This conflict merged with other disagreements over the succeeding years. As a result, the Lower House refused to pass any taxing authorization for the South Carolina colony during the remaining years of that colony's existence.[68]

The British government's heavy-handed rejection of the South Carolina's Lower House appropriation, in the face of years of precedent to the contrary, helped turn some modest, English-loving colonists into new patriots. Once they became convinced that a British government conspiracy was under way to deny them their liberty, they were not bashful in criticizing the king's ministers for determined actions to enslave all Americans. The irony of the fact that some of these new South Carolina patriots, passionate to resist British policies designed to "enslave" them, were themselves slave owners seemed to have been lost to them. They lacked the open honesty of men such as George Washington, who admitted the hypocrisy of slave owners calling for personal liberty.

The Wilkes affair gave substance to political ideas and theoretical propositions that had been circulating throughout the colonies for some time. Those ideas were the counterparts of the religious revivals that elevated the lives of so many ordinary colonists. They were the intellectual's activity in clearing a field of stones and stumps, and plowing it in preparation for the seeds of liberty, for that idea of liberty became a persistent theme in the decade following the French and Indian War.

Thoughtful people, be they patriots or conservatives, had an abiding concern for "liberty." Some of the major tracts on liberty came out of the English turmoil surrounding the Glorious Revolution of 1688-89—a relatively peaceful revolution, when Parliament forced King James II from the throne, as well as from England, and installed William and Mary as the new monarch. Those revolutionary ideas circulating through England in the late 1680s continued simmering through the British political communities.

At the start of the 1720s, John Trenchard and Thomas Gordon popularized ideas from the Glorious Revolution again. The two men were journalists, or publicists. They took ideas found in philosophical writings, such as John Locke's and Algeron Sidney's, and made them understandable to those common people who had been fortunate enough to learn to read in their youth. Not long after Trenchard and Gordon began publishing The Independent Whig, copies could be found in America.[69]

The Independent Whig lasted for fifty-three issues, starting in 1719, and ending in 1720. One of the writers' pleas was for recognizing Protestant dissenters' rights in the midst of the established Church of England. These arguments carried special resonance when colonial printers reprinted them during the early decades of the Great Awakening (1740s and '50s), but Trenchard and Gordon's most persistent theme was a plea on behalf of liberty.[70]

Perhaps seeking a wider audience, the two men issued a series of essays through the London Journal, starting near the end of 1720. They signed their essays "Cato" to signify their allegiance to liberty. In the time of the Roman republic, Cato had been an influential opponent of Julius Caesar's grasp of dictatorial power.[71]

Trenchard and Gordon wrote over 130 "Cato" essays, ranging in focus from corruption in government to the value of liberty, the threat of tyranny to the dangers of High Churchmen. The man holding the prime minister's post took offense at their effective criticism of him, and bribed the London Journal's publisher to discontinue criticisms of the government and instead print defenses of governmental policy. The Journal stopped publishing Cato in September 1722. Even so, both The Independent Whig and "Cato's Letters" continued to be popular. Versions of each were reprinted in England into the 1750s, and printers in both New York and Philadelphia made copies. Not only did John Adams and Thomas Jefferson have copies in their personal libraries, but the publications were found in America's college libraries, in public or "subscription" libraries, and in bookstores in several colonial cities in the years preceding the Revolution. Newspaper columnists quoted them regularly, or, more conveniently, plagiarized them in their essays.[72]

Josiah Quincy Sr. demonstrated the importance thoughtful patriots gave to ideas: to exploring ideas, arguing over them, melding them into new ideas, and eventually converting them from the ideas of others to ideas they personally advanced. In February 1774, Quincy wrote his will. In it, he bestowed upon his son: "Algeron Sidney's works,—John Locke's works,—Lord Bacon's works,—Gordon's Tacitus,—and Cato's Letters." He wished his son might find that "the spirit of liberty [would] rest upon him."[73]

Often, the issue colonial essayists addressed was the threat "Power" posed to "Liberty." Liberty was described as passive and delicate; power as hungry and aggressive. Power was often depicted as having "an encroaching nature." While power was a legitimate component of good government, essayists saw the human element causing an abuse of power. They believed that unchecked human nature naturally would tend toward lust, the enhancement of personal or institutional power, and corruption. Hence Quincy's wish that his son gain an abiding devotion to liberty. Checks had to be built into all governmental systems to protect the people from the aggressive use of power and the corresponding loss of liberty.[74]

All that was very nice theory, but what did it mean in practice? Thoughtful colonists believed they had at least some of the answers. And in coming up with the answers they were tilling the soil in order to plant real seeds of liberty.

At base was a commitment to "the constitution." By this colonists meant not a framework for government, such as the US Constitution, but rather the British government itself, and the laws, traditions, and customs shaping it. Within government, balances and checks served to restrain the aggressive use of power and protect the essential component of a well-regulated, happy society: liberty.

Let conniving men overturn the balance or run roughshod over the checks, and tyranny, or "slavery," resulted. Power sharing was one of the important checks within the British constitution: royalty (the Monarchy), the aristocracy (the House of Lords), and the populace (the House of Commons). Theoretically, their voluntary sharing of power kept tyranny in check. Should that check prove inadequate, then an independent judiciary stood ready to protect liberty.[75]

All constitutions were susceptible to subversion. Colonists frequently referenced the fate of classical Denmark as such an example. But they saw the abiding spirit of liberty in the British people as the great bulwark against tyranny in the mother country. Yes, Charles I brought tyranny to the nation, but liberty-loving men—both lords and commoners—rose to liberty's defense, and Charles lost his head. James II followed suit a few decades after. Again, lords and commons negotiated with William of Orange to force James II from the throne. Then, lords and commons sought to blunt a future monarch's power-grab. They established a new sharing of power in which Parliament seemingly gained ascendancy over the Crown. This was designed to provide greater protection for liberty than had been possible when the Monarch was supreme.

The Massachusetts Bay Charter of 1691 was the natural product of the Glorious Revolution that overthrew James II and brought in William and Mary as monarchs, but under parliamentary authority. Royal charters written before 1688 established colonial governments in which the legislature's lower house was popularly elected but the Crown appointed both the upper house/governor's council and the governor. In Massachusetts Bay, under the charter of 1691, both lower and upper houses were elected, restricting Crown authority to the appointed governor, justices on the superior court, sheriffs and justices of the peace. In local government, taxpayers controlled the town meetings, the most powerful unit of local government. Thus, theoretically, power was balanced and liberty protected.[76]

Of course, the colonies still were subservient to Parliament. This condition occasionally proved uncomfortable for individual colonies as clashes of interest arose. Most of those disagreements eventually were resolved and colonies resumed constructive relations with the mother country.

The era of the French and Indian War (1754-63) became a watershed in regard to trans-Atlantic relations. During that time, some colonial legislatures worked hard to provide both soldiers and material aid, and vigorously supported the war effort. Others were intermittently cooperative. A few simply ignored the war because it did not directly involve them. In economic matters, some merchants made huge profits by supplying French forces with essential materials. They smuggled those goods into Canada, thus helping the French in Canada survive, and so prolonging the war.

When the war ended, parliamentary leaders looked at the colonies and drew two conclusions. One was that the colonies had been allowed too much flexibility in setting their governmental and economic policies. The second was that the colonies derived benefits from the war in the form of France's removal from North America, and now they should share the war's continuing cost, as well as the expense of maintaining an army in the colonies, whether colonists wanted a British army in their midst or not.[77]

Some colonial newspapers printed negative political arguments, and sermons that carried political implications often were published, but the intellectual climate within the colonies generally had supported the British government. Parliament's passage of two oppressive acts: the Sugar Act and, more ominously, the Stamp Act, changed that.

Daniel Dulany came to Maryland in 1703 as an indentured servant, though he had studied law in London. Subsequent to his servitude he made great strides in the province as a lawyer. Dulany had a son, Daniel Dulany the Younger, who followed in his father's footsteps. After classical studies at Cambridge, young Dulany studied law at London's Middle Temple.

Back in Maryland, Dulany the Younger's legal star rose quickly, as did his political and social status. Though well disposed toward the British government, when Parliament passed the Stamp

Act, Dulany the Younger's thoughts on liberty quickly turned him to fear parliamentary tyranny. He recorded those thoughts in "Considerations on the Propriety of Imposing Taxes in the British Colonies, For the Purpose of Raising a Revenue, By Act of Parliament." Published in Annapolis, copies soon were being read up and down the colonies.[78]

Dulany acknowledged Parliament's supremacy over the colonies, a position he never relinquished. But he made a clear distinction between parliamentary oversight of colonies and its levying taxes on colonists for raising revenue. "It is an essential principle of the English constitution that the subject [i.e.: individual] shall not be taxed without his consent." Realizing that some in England advanced the theory of "virtual representation," he proceeded to demolish such misconception. Under the virtual representation theory, members of Parliament did not represent a specific geographical location, but rather each member actually represented virtually all English citizens, wherever they lived. That, of course, included all those who (or whose ancestors) emigrated from England to the colonies.[79]

Members of the House of Commons, Dulany commented, might argue reasonably that they represented all citizens of England, including those living in cities from which no member of the House was elected, such as Leeds or Birmingham, because those un-represented residents were "neighbors" of voters whose interests and concerns were similar to their own. Colonists, by contrast, had no neighbors with representation in Parliament. For Americans, advancing the "notion of virtual representation…is a mere cob-web, spread to catch the unwary, and to entangle the weak."[80]

Dulany reminded his readers that colonists were not immune from tax burdens. But those taxes imposed upon them legitimately could come from just one source. "The colonies have a complete and adequate legislative authority, and are not only represented in their assemblies, but in no other manner."[81]

While Parliament was the supreme legislature in the Empire, if it had exceeded the constitution in passing the Stamp Act, how could the colonies both honor parliamentary supremacy and at the same time assert their constitutional right to be taxed only by their duly elected representatives? Dulany counseled "prudence, as well as duty, requires submission." Meanwhile, "We ought with spirit, and vigour, and alacrity, to bid defiance to tyranny, by exposing its impotence. ... By a vigorous application to manufactures, the consequence of oppression in the colonies to the inhabitants of Great Britain, would strike home, immediately." In other words, counter the political war with an economic war: stop buying British goods, replace them with locally produced goods, and England's working populace, seeing their jobs disappear, will demand that Parliament rescind the Stamp tax.

Dulany was not a voice in the wilderness. Other colonists wrote essays or had their letters attacking parliamentary taxation printed in colonial newspapers. Delegates from nine colonies joined in the Stamp Act Congress to protest the tax and petition the king and Parliament. So there was a healthy mix of ideas. In fact, colonists' protests had moved several steps beyond the appeals for reason made in response to the Sugar Act. Stamp Act protests included the Congress involving nine colonies, and then creation of collaborative economic warfare in the form of boycotts of British goods.[82]

Not content with the niceties of formal protests, economic pressure, and humble petitions, patriot leaders in several colonies used mob force to secure the resignations of those the British government had designated as stamp distributors.[83]

Parliament eventually receded from colonists' verbal and economic assaults and repealed the Stamp Act without its ever being enforced. Before doing so, Parliament passed the "Declaratory Act," claiming for itself authority to legislate for the colonies "in all cases whatsoever." When asked whether this Declaratory Act gave Parliament taxing power over the colonies, Dulany's training in British law held him in good stead. He noted that a Declaratory Act passed with respect to Ireland during the reign of George I did not claim taxing authority for Parliament. Since Parliament had no taxing authority over Ireland, he said, it could have none over the colonies.[84]

As the debate and the economic contest moved forward, another colonist argued for repeal of the Stamp Act. He did so privately, in a letter to a prominent parliamentary leader. John Dickinson, one of Pennsylvania's foremost lawyers, sent his letter to London in December 1765, pleading the colonies' case. British leaders, he suggested, might suppose the colonies were too jealous and suspicious of each other to cooperate, and assume adversity would not be sufficient for the colonies to unite in opposition to Parliament. Such suspicions and intercolonial economic battles were real but faded into insignificance when colonies faced tyrannical power. "No colony apprehends that any other has Designs upon its Liberty. Their Contests are of an inferior Nature, and will vanish when one more dreadful to them commences." As he demonstrated a decade later in the Continental Congress, John Dickinson sought liberty within the Empire, not independence. Yet, committed as he was to British loyalty, he realized that British tyranny might force the colonies toward independence. He wanted one of Britain's most respected politicians to understand that love of liberty came before loyalty to the Crown.

Others were not to be so restrained in their thoughts.[85]

For a time—a short time—following Parliament's repeal of the Stamp Act, relations between most of the colonies and Parliament were relatively placid. Then along came Charles Townshend and the theory that duties levied on imports into the colonies really were not taxes, even if their purpose was raising revenue rather than regulating trade. The Townshend Duties generated a new spate of arguments regarding parliamentary authority over the colonies. This time, John Dickinson put on his public face and prepared a series of statements opposing parliamentary taxation. While still acknowledging Great Britain's supremacy over the colonies, he moved the debate further along the lines of colonial political independence.

John Dickinson was a highly successful lawyer in Philadelphia. He was well read in British law and history, having studied in London at the Middle Temple. Yet he also understood how to draw in and persuade a lay audience, for he issued his statements through newspapers as "Letters from a Farmer in Pennsylvania." (Perhaps his wife planted a garden behind their mansion.) In these "Letters," along with other widely read documents, Dickinson advanced some new ideas.

The "Letters" were an immediate hit, and were republished in all but four colonial newspapers. Some English newspapers also copied the letters, giving them favorable commentaries. They went through further editions as pamphlets.[86]

The Townshend Duties were unconstitutional taxes on the colonies, Dickinson asserted. It mattered not that they were import duties, and therefore "external" taxes, rather than the "internal" taxes that the Stamp Tax levied. They were simply a different, unconstitutional version of that unconstitutional Stamp Act.

Stating fundamental principles, Dickinson argued that colonists were, in fact, Englishmen. As such, they were guaranteed under the constitution the right of taxing themselves. But he went further. Englishmen carried with them, wherever they went, the right of self-government. And that right could only be secured if it were based on a government acting within limited powers: "For WHO ARE A FREE PEOPLE? Not those, over whom government is reasonable and equitably exercised, but those, who live under a government so constitutionally checked and controlled, that proper provision is made against its being otherwise exercised."

The Townshend Duties were every bit as odious a tax on American colonists as had been the Stamp Act. (And Dickinson was thoroughly familiar with that attempt to tax the colonists, for he had been a delegate to the Stamp Act Congress.) He reiterated the position that it made no difference that these duties were "external" rather than "internal" taxes. Also, the relatively small taxes imposed on each imported item made no difference. They were an unconstitutional infringement of colonists' rights:

> These duties…are expressly laid FOR THE SOLE PURPOSE OF TAKING MONEY. This is the true definition of "taxes." They are therefore taxes. This money is to be taken from us. We are therefore taxed. Those who are taxed without their own consent, expressed by themselves or their representatives, are slaves.

He went on to argue that colonists were tied to the British government through affection: "A dependence founded on mutual benefits, the continuance of which can be secured only by mutual affections."

While stressing the need to guard their constitutional rights against the incursions of oppressive ministers, Dickinson reminded his readers that a united defense increased their chances of guarding those rights successfully. American colonies' "prosperity does not depend on ministerial favors doled out to particular provinces," Dickinson argued. "They [the American colonies] form one political body, of which each colony is a member. Their happiness is founded on their constitution; and is to be promoted, by preserving that constitution in unabated vigor, throughout every part."[87]

Massachusetts Governor Francis Bernard grudgingly recognized the potency of Dickinson's arguments in building colonial resistance to the Townshend Acts. He observed that Dickinson had formulated "a Bill of Rights in the Opinion of the Americans." He forecast that "Parliament may enact declaratory Acts as many as they please; but they must not expect any real obedience." In this regard, Governor Bernard might well have quoted Dickinson directly, for the "Farmer" noted that Americans were "as much dependent on Great Britain as one free people could be on another."[88]

Dickinson's persuasive "Letters" galvanized many Whig critics of the British government into action. They busied themselves with a new burst of letters and essays attacking the Townshend Duties as well as local conditions that they saw as threatening colonists' liberty. Not surprisingly, one of these writers was Boston's leading radical patriot, Samuel Adams.

Having capped off his academic studies in 1743 with a master's degree from Harvard in what we today would call political science, Sam Adams learned over the years to cast his writing style to appeal to the layperson rather than the academic expert. In 1768 he pondered the relationship—if any—between Parliament and colonial legislatures. All (British and colonial) legislative authority, he said, must maintain self-restraint, because it could not "overleap without destroying its own foundation." There was a higher authority that every legislature must acknowledge and respect: the British constitution, a constitution that "is fixed" and has as its base "the law of God and nature." While Parliament might be the supreme legislature within the British Empire, and the colonial legislatures might be subordinate to it, neither the supreme nor subordinate legislature could legitimately extend its jurisdiction beyond the bounds of the constitution founded on the "law of God and nature." Such a foundation protected colonists from parliamentary interference because "an essential natural right [is] that a man shall quietly enjoy and have the sole disposal of his property." Since colonists voluntarily gave assent to their elected representatives in their colonial legislatures to tax them and otherwise administer their government to the colonists' benefit, Parliament had no right to override that legislature.[89]

Dickinson's arguments, and those of likeminded penmen such as Sam Adams, aimed at using reason to persuade the mass of people to stand up for colonial liberties, while other Whig attacks emphasized emotional appeals. Here the British government lent a hand.

Boston protests against the Stamp Act had been particularly violent and destructive. This, coupled with other disturbances, led British officials to detach a body of troops to the Massachusetts

Bay capital. Once news of the troops' impending arrival became public, patriot papers issued a drumbeat of criticism.

Andrew Eliot offered this in September 1768: "Good God! What can be worse to a people who have tasted the sweets of liberty!" Eliot then warned: "Things have come to an unhappy crisis; there will never be that harmony between Great Britain and her colonies that there hath been; all confidence is at an end; and the moment there is any blood shed all affection will cease." Yet such criticism was relatively mild compared with the campaign organized and maintained after the troops settled into Boston.[90]

Starting in September 1768, and continuing for over ten months, a dedicated group of patriot propagandists in Boston wrote weekly issues of a "JOURNAL OF OCCURRENCES." This "Journal" chronicled alleged insults, assaults, abuses, and even rapes British troops, or "Lobster Backs" (so called for the red uniform jackets the troops wore), committed against innocent young women, kindly old ladies, or professional men. The authors ridiculed the troops as "conservators of the peace."[91]

While publicists wrote the "Journal" in Boston, it appeared first in a New York newspaper a week or more after its posted date. It then was copied in many other colonial newspapers. The Boston edition usually was printed a month after the datemark. This meant, according to Lieutenant Governor Thomas Hutchinson, that none of the incidents could be verified since the elapsed time made checking on them all but impossible.

The authors of these articles seemed to have two purposes in mind. One, of course, was to rid the town of the troops. The other was to drive Governor Bernard out of office. The articles did not by themselves succeed in forcing Bernard to leave. He did, in fact, return to England, sailing on August 1, 1769, a thoroughly beaten man. With his departure, the "Journal" ceased publication. The troops stayed, but when a volley of Redcoat fire killed five civilians on March 5, 1770, Governor Hutchinson, under pressure from Boston's political leaders, evacuated the troops to Castle William in Boston harbor.[92]

That event also reminded patriots of the trouble the New York assembly found itself in a few years earlier. Following riots associated with the Stamp Act protests, General Gage, commander of British troops in America, moved several detachments to Albany and New York City from western frontiers where they had been responding to Indian uprisings. Parliament had passed a Quartering Act in 1765, specifying the material support colonial governments were required to provide when troops were stationed there. Gage asked New York's legislature for that support.

At first refusing to acknowledge the Quartering Act's legitimacy, the Assembly approved some funds, but not all the act had stipulated. Gage accepted this. Later, when additional troops arrived, he again sought support. The Assembly charged that the Quartering Act was a tax on colonists and therefore was as unconstitutional as the Stamp Act. While authorizing some funds, it refused to provide all the act stipulated. The dispute poured over to Parliament. It settled the matter.

Overturning the long-held Royal prerogative of determining (through the Crown's agent in the colonies, the Royal Governor) when colonial legislatures are called to sit and when they are prorogued or dissolved, Parliament shut down the New York Assembly. It forbade the Assembly to pass any legislation until the Assembly met all stipulated requirements set forth in the Quartering Act.[93]

A new form of parliamentary tyranny! Clearly an unconstitutional assault on colonists' rights, said many pundits. Although Parliament's exercise of raw political power forced New York's Assembly to comply with the Quartering Act's dictates, stories of this action were added to the already seething cauldron of discontent and protest in the colonies. "If our legislative authority can be suspended whenever we refuse obedience to laws we never consented to, we may as well...acknowledge ourselves slaves," wrote a correspondent to the Boston Gazette in August 1767.[94]

Patriot leaders in Boston sought to widen political resistance to Parliament by proposing that the legislature send a circular letter to legislatures in all the colonies. They suggested the letter promote cooperation in resisting parliamentary encroachment of American rights. To the patriots' mortification, the lower house rejected the idea. Governor Bernard was ecstatic! About the same time he received a letter from the Secretary of State for the Southern Colonies (which included North America), in which the Secretary approved the governor's recent actions thwarting some patriot initiatives and censuring the popular party for some intemperate statements. Governor Bernard promptly sent the Secretary's letter to be read to the assembly.[95]

Perhaps motivated by the Secretary's attacks, the patriots asked and received from the assembly permission to reconsider the proposed circular letter. Not only did a majority now endorse preparing the letter, it also agreed to erase from the record the earlier rejection.[96]

The Speaker of the Lower House sent the circular letter to the speakers of the other colonial legislatures. He also had it published in the Boston Gazette. Maintaining that Parliament's taxes on the colonists gave them a common worry, he suggested that legislative leaders should "harmonize with each other." While acknowledging parliamentary supremacy over the Empire, the Massachusetts speaker maintained this did not give Parliament unbridled power, because "in all free states the constitution is fixed." Parliament could not go beyond its duly constituted authority "without destroying its own foundation. ..." Americans enjoyed the benefits of "an essential, unalterable right of nature, engrafted into the British constitution, as a fundamental law" that citizens could not have their property taken from them without their consent. Americans, he said, "assert this natural and constitutional right." Although the Speaker acknowledged the king as "our common head and father," this was simply a concluding flourish.[97]

Virginia's legislature was most prominent in responding positively to the letter. It, in turn, sent out a circular letter to the other legislative leaders. Most other colonies offered positive responses; though the Quaker-dominated Pennsylvania legislature simply had the letter read to its members and went on with other business.

Back in London, the government was in some turmoil, with elections scheduled and uncontrolled riots spewing forth across London. The king was unhappy with the (colonial) Secretary's work and wanted him out but was unwilling to say so. As a result, the government chose to divide the duties he performed, creating a new cabinet post of Secretary of State for America. The Earl of Hillsborough, a man who intensely disliked the American colonists and believed they should be brought to heel, took that post. He quickly gave the patriots new kindling to fuel the fire of liberty.[98]

The new Secretary for America's view of the colonies, while more extreme than some members of the British government, epitomized the intellectual rigidity a majority of Parliament held, and certainly represented King George III's views. The colonies were subservient to Parliament; colonial legislatures held no more power than municipal corporations; parliamentary dictates were not open to negotiation, only to obedience. Almost immediately, he put these attitudes and views into policy.[99]

Having read a report from Governor Bernard concerning the Massachusetts legislature's adoption of a circular letter, the Secretary wrote Bernard that such legislative action was to be reversed. Bernard was to require the legislature to rescind the circular letter and apologize for having prepared it. Should the legislature refuse, Bernard was ordered to dissolve the legislature and send a copy of the proceedings to the Parliament. The Secretary's goal was to thwart future efforts to create measures of "so extraordinary and unconstitutional a nature."[100]

As might well be expected from the unfolding story, the Massachusetts legislature demanded that Governor Bernard provide a copy of the Secretary's letter. When Bernard sent the letter over, the legislature voted ninety-two to seventeen against rescinding the circular letter. Before Bernard was able to dissolve the legislature, the assembly also excoriated Bernard, telling the king in a petition for Bernard's removal from office, that the governor was guilty of innumerable political crimes. To add to Bernard's woes the upper house joined the assembly in petitioning for Bernard's removal.[101]

Not content with attacking the Massachusetts legislature, the Secretary wrote a circular letter to all the governors, telling them to see that their legislatures responded to the Massachusetts legislature's circular letter with "contempt." Should the legislatures actually consider that letter, the governors were to prorogue or dissolve their legislature immediately. Up and down the Atlantic coast, when the Secretary's circular letter was delivered to colonial legislatures, they acted predictably, as did the governors. Like a row of dominoes, legislature after legislature rejected this threat to its independence and found its governor knocking it down. Even the passive Quaker members of the Pennsylvania legislature realized their liberty was at risk and declared they had a right to correspond with those in other legislatures. The Quaker legislators now contended that they, not Parliament, held the constitutional power to tax their own citizens. So, pacifism had its limits.[102]

The Secretary for America demanded colonial conformity to government dictate; the colonial legislatures maintained their independence. Essayists and enthusiastic patriots used both the Massachusetts legislature's defiance and their own colony's legislative show of independence to reiterate the growing colonial maturity in political thought. In a spirit that was perhaps more emotional than intellectual, when new elections in South Carolina were called in 1769, "mechanics" in Charleston held a massive rally. They declared a large oak tree to be a "Tree of Liberty," sang a patriotic song John Dickinson had written, then decorated the tree with forty-five lights, fired forty-five rockets, lit forty-five candles and carried them to the governor's house where they toasted the "Massachusetts Ninety-two." After this, they retired to a local tavern and enjoyed forty-five bowls of wine, forty-five bowls of punch, and used ninety-two glasses, all illumined by forty-five candles. Similar expressions of admiration and support for Wilkes and for the "Massachusetts 92" took place in many communities throughout 1769. Clearly, the spirit of liberty was thriving.[103]

These activities sponsored by groups of mechanics and others of the "middling sort" gave credence to contentions that newspaper and pamphlet arguments in defense of liberty were influencing people's behavior. Challenges to growing British threats against colonists' governmental authority were not simply floating on high among the relatively small number of colonial intellectual elite. They were being studied and digested by thousands of working people as well.

Through private letters merchants, lawyers, and politicians in America sent to counterparts in England, the growing strength of opinion regarding colonial resistance to domineering governmental policies reached the ears of those in power in London. Yet these statements, and the accompanying advice, generated no change in governmental attitude. Accept your subservient position, bow to parliamentary supremacy, conform to London's dictates, or suffer the consequences seemed to epitomize the cabinet members' position.[104]

Americans had made their theoretical and constitutional cases. But they did not stop there. As with the Stamp Act resistance, patriots organized an intercolonial boycott to resist the Townshend Duties. Not surprisingly, many newspapers encouraged this. The colonies were in a recession. Newspapers could hardly afford to raise their subscription rates. Yet under the Townshend Act, paper imported from England was taxed. American entrepreneurs made very little paper, so the newspaper publishers had no choice but to pay the tax on the paper and thus increase the risk of failure with their rising cost.[105]

Gradually, patriots persuaded local merchants to join in a general boycott of British goods, and another test of parliamentary endurance. Public pressure was the usual approach to securing reluctant merchants' compliance, but patriots did not eschew the application of force. Professions of a love of liberty and the protection of freedom did not keep ardent patriots from violating those claims when forcing recalcitrant merchants to conform to patriot desires.[106]

Whether the boycotts were effective in pressuring Parliament to rescind the taxes continues to be debated, with the negative assessment having the greater support, but in 1770 Parliament rescinded all the Townshend Duties except the tea tax. The colonies settled down to another tranquil interlude in their relations with the mother country.

During this period politically astute colonists resumed reading classical and historical works relating to political philosophy and continued sharing ideas with each other. Patriots who were inclined to action chafed at the growing interaction between colonial merchants and their counterparts in Britain. These patriots looked around for new opportunities to bring pressure on Parliament to recognize American rights.

Parliament provided the opportunity patriots sought when it passed the Tea Act.

V

The Incident at Griffin's Wharf

Though a cold rain was falling, they came in droves—some from nearby, others from neighboring towns, a few from as far as twenty miles away. They gathered at Boston's Old South Meeting church for the ten o'clock meeting on December 16, 1773. About two thousand protesters arrived from Brookline, Cambridge, Charleston, Dorchester, Weston, and other towns. These joined with around three thousand Bostonians to hear the latest news about the tea. The crowd was so large it overflowed into the street.

Plans for this meeting had been in the works for days. In fact, large gatherings had come together at Faneuil Hall the preceding two days to discuss the quandary caused when neither British authorities in Boston nor patriot leaders could fashion a compromise agreeable to both. Now, the presence of men from towns some distance outside Boston gave significant support to local patriot leaders. In fact, the Boston Committee of Correspondence, first organized in 1772, had been in communication with similar committees throughout Massachusetts almost from its founding. In response, committees from Cambridge, Brookline, Roxbury, Charlestown, Marblehead, Plymouth, Malden, Gloucester, Lexington, Groton, Newburyport, Lynn, and Medford wrote to the Boston Committee, pledging their support for Boston, all in advance of this fateful day.[107]

Thousands of people were here because the tea contained in the holds of three vessels carried with it a plague: the British Parliament's three-pence-per-pound tax on tea imported to America. That was an illegal tax, as far as many American colonists were concerned, because it was levied on them without their consent. Under the British constitution, citizens' property (in this case money) could not be taken from them in the form of taxes, except by action of their duly elected representatives. American colonists were not, and could not be, represented in Parliament. Only colonial legislatures, whose members colonists elected, could tax their citizens, these protesters were saying.

The question of the day—that is, December 16—was whether the tea was to be landed and the tax paid, whether it was to be returned to England, or what.

After the crowd settled down and formal preliminaries were completed, Francis Rotch became the center of attention. Representing his family, which owned the ship Dartmouth, young Rotch already had been through tough times with members of the Boston Committee of Correspondence, with officials of the customs collector's office, as well as with a British naval officer.[108]

The Dartmouth was the first of three ships to come into Boston Harbor from Britain carrying East India Company tea. It had arrived on Saturday, November 27, 1773. Those at the meeting wanted to know if the Dartmouth and, presumably, the other two ships, one of which the Rotch family also owned, would return to England with the tea in their holds before customs officials claimed the cargo for nonpayment of the hated Townshend tea tax.

Rotch told the crowd that both the customs commissioner and a naval official had refused him clearance to depart until the tea duty was paid. He also explained that British warships in the harbor would not let him pass without clearance. Indeed, warships had been moved to cover not only the main channel but also the smaller channels which coastal sloops sometimes used. Furthermore, even if he were to evade such a formidable challenge, he could be ruined financially if he tried to return the tea to England without documentation, for to do so would violate British law.

Keeping Rotch under intense pressure, those in charge told him he had one more hoop to jump. He must go to Governor Hutchinson personally and ask for a permit to depart. The problem: Hutchinson had fled Boston for his country home in Milton, some seven miles away, to avoid possible Boston mob threats. Rotch was given until three o'clock that afternoon to reach Milton, confer with Governor Hutchinson, and return with the governor's decision. Meeting managers appointed a delegation to accompany him. The meeting's leaders knew that the governor's council and many members of the legislature's lower house already had advised the governor to allow the tea to be returned to Britain, without the tax being paid. No doubt they also believed that Governor Hutchinson was thoroughly familiar with the substantial—and sincere—efforts men of various classes and opinions had made to have the tea returned to England safely. Numerous meetings toward that end had been held. A knowledgeable person reported about one such meeting: "The moderator and people were strongly desirous of preserving the tea untouched for the East India Company.... They insisted, therefore, that it should go back in the same bottoms."[109]

The December 16 morning meeting adjourned until midafternoon.

Three o'clock came with the crowd eager to hear what Governor Hutchinson had decided. But Rotch was not present. As time dragged on, the audience became restive. Prominent patriots spoke and proposed various resolutions for those in attendance to pass while waiting for Rotch's return. Still he did not appear. At five in the evening, a vote was called to adjourn the meeting. Several pleaded for more time and managed to gain another hour.

Finally, about 5:45 p.m., Rotch arrived. Speaking by candlelight, for in December night falls early in northern latitudes, Rotch reported that Governor Hutchinson rejected his appeal for a pass to allow Dartmouth to leave with the tea in its hold. And at midnight the twenty-day grace period would end for paying the tea tax. If it were not paid, customs officials would confiscate the tea and remove it, probably to Castle William on a fortified island in the harbor.

After hearing Rotch's report, followed by several fiery comments from others, Sam Adams rose and announced to the crowd: "this meeting can do nothing further to save the country." A whoop rose from men in the gallery; a similar cry came from some stationed outside the Meeting House. Soon, bands of "Mohawks," that is men who had decorated themselves with Indian makeup or, in some cases, simply smeared soot on their faces, headed for Griffin's wharf.[110]

According to eyewitnesses, the "Mohawks" knew what they were about and were careful to limit their activities to removing the tea and dumping it into Boston harbor. "The impression was that of solemnity, rather than of riot and confusion."[111]

They did not have an easy task. The "Mohawks" first divided themselves into three groups, each taking one of the vessels: Dartmouth, Eleanor, and Beaver. Once on board they used block and tackle to raise the heavy, lead-lined chests—averaging more than three hundred pounds gross weight each—from the hold to the deck. Then hatchets came into play to open the chests. Finally, the "Mohawks" pushed tea and the chests overboard into the harbor. Some men also were assigned guard duty to see that those watching the event did not steal any of the tea for personal use.

The complexity of hauling heavy chests out of the holds, then opening and disgorging their contents, required some knowledge and experience in handling ships' cargo. In fact, reviewing the lists of men believed to have participated in the Tea Party, somewhere between a dozen and twenty men may have had direct experience working around the docks or on board ships.[112]

Curiously, the wielding of guns was not prominent during the episode, yet a local resident merchant, John Andrews, had commented that all the guns in Boston's shops had disappeared prior to the December 16 gathering. Speculating that citizens were preparing to resist if troops from Castle William were brought to town to cow residents into submission, he observed that the guns were "all bought up, with a full determination to repell force by force." But soldiers remained on the island because Governor Thomas Hutchinson did not ask for help in keeping order.[113]

Fortunately for the "Indians," the rain which had been falling all day had stopped and the clouds parted, leaving a dim moonlit night which was enhanced by many lanterns individuals had brought along. Still, completing the task required strenuous work, for among the three ships were 340 chests holding some 90,000 pounds of tea. For accountants in the crowd, this was valued at £9,000.[114]

Perhaps because the "Mohawk" leaders were both skilled and disciplined, there was very little collateral damage. In two of the three vessels cargo other than tea brought over from Britain already had been unloaded. The brig, the last of the vessels to arrive, still had its cargo in the hold. A leader of the "Mohawk" band told the captain they would work around the other freight and take only the tea.

Unlike earlier action in Boston where mobs destroyed or damaged houses and businesses, those involved in the tea party appeared to work under strict discipline. In fact, when a padlock was broken and then found to belong to a ship's captain, someone replaced the lock.[115]

By nine o'clock, all the chests had been dumped in the harbor and the decks cleared. Somewhere around 110 to 120 men had accomplished the heavy work. (Efforts made several decades later to identify the willing workers produced a few names, of whom three were prominent patriots in December 1773. They were merchant William Molineux, Dr. Thomas Young, and the engraver and silversmith Paul Revere. Certainly, neither Sam Adams nor John Hancock took part in the formal Tea Party.)

Some days after the party, when government officials attempted to identify those involved, none of the large crowd watching the show would admit to having recognized any of the "Indians."

The next day one of those almost certainly involved in the previous night's tea removal, Paul Revere, was in the saddle, carrying reports to New York City which Sam Adams had prepared. He reached the city on December 21. Copies of Adams's dispatch went on to Philadelphia. From there the news was sent south to Charleston.[116]

A few days after the tea party, most of Boston's merchants agreed not to sell tea after January 20, 1774. When that day arrived, two barrels of unsold tea were placed in front of the customs house and set on fire.

Governor Hutchinson wrote official reports to Lord Dartmouth (the second person to hold the position of Secretary of State for America since that cabinet post had been established) and to the East India Company. Others in Boston wrote friends or business associates in London, and copies of Boston newspaper articles were packed up quickly and sent to London newspapers. The first of these communications arrived in London on January 19, 1774, some five weeks after the event.[117]

Reactions among colonists to this daring and dramatic act of defiance predictably were varied, though individuals in Massachusetts offering negative comments generally kept them close to home. One critic of the patriot action did put his thoughts on paper. He was Peter Oliver, Chief Justice of the Massachusetts Superior Court and brother of Lieutenant Governor Andrew Oliver.

> Leaders of the Faction, assembled the Rabble in the largest Dissenting Meeting House in the Town, where they had frequently assembled to pronounce their Annual Orations upon their Massacre, & to perpetuate their most atrocious Acts of Treason & Rebellion—thus, literally, "turning the House of God into a Den of Thieves."

Oliver went on to describe the men breaking open the tea chests and pouring the tea into the harbor. He then noted ironically:

> Had they have been prudent enough to have poured it into fresh Water instead of Salt Water, they & their Wives, & their Children, & their little-ones, might have regaled upon it, at free Cost, for a twelve Month; but now the Fish had the whole Regale to themselves... it is said, that some of the Inhabitants of Boston would not eat of Fish caught in their Harbor, because they had drunk of the East India Tea.[118]

John Adams expressed a thoughtful Patriot view the day after the tea party when he wrote in his diary:

> Last night 3 Cargoes of Bohea Tea were emptied into the Sea.... This is the most magnificent Movement of all. There is a Dignity, a Majesty, a Sublimity, in this last Effort of the Patriots, that I greatly admire. The People should never rise, without doing something to be remembered—something notable and striking. This Destruction of the Tea is so bold, so daring, so firm, intrepid and inflexible, and it must have so important Consequences, and so lasting, that I can't but consider it as an Epocha in History.

Adams did not limit himself to celebratory thoughts. He went on to ask:

> What measures will the Ministry take, in Consequence of this?— Will they resent it? will they dare to resent it? will they punish Us? How? By quartering Troops upon Us?— by annulling our Charter?—by laying on more duties? By restraining our Trade? By Sacrifice of Individuals, or how.[119]

Governor Thomas Hutchinson realized he had to defend his inaction on the event. He wrote to Lord Dartmouth that so many men of property and prominence, including John Hancock, the wealthiest person in the colony, were present at the fateful meeting preceding the tea party, there seemed little likelihood any untoward action would be sanctioned (and, in fact, the meeting did not sanction the tea's destruction). By that time, Hutchinson said he had done all he could to protect the tea. The designated tea consignees had offered to pay the tax and store the tea in a safe place, but the patriots had rejected that proposal. Then the governor had offered to allow the ships to be moved away from Griffin's wharf and put under the Royal Navy's protection. Rotch rejected that alternative (probably realizing to do so would place him at odds with patriot leaders). Hutchinson then considered having a Royal Navy ship move in and remove the tea ships from the wharf but thought he did not have authority to do so on his own, and believed the governor's council would not countenance such action.

Hutchinson might have ordered marines to go on the tea ships to overpower the patriots who were guarding the ships. Such action, he thought, would lead to bloodshed, which then would mean having the soldiers on Castle William Island come to the aid of the marines. He considered the number of troops stationed there insufficient to take control of all Boston, so those actions seemed likely to be counterproductive.

Since customs and naval officials had refused to issue clearance papers, the only way for a peaceful resolution of the impasse was for the governor to sign a pass to allow the tea-laden ships to leave Boston for a return voyage to England. Hutchinson said doing that would violate Massachusetts law, and also would authorize the return of the tea to England in violation of British law. Therefore, he did nothing.[120]

Couldn't a governor claim authority to act independently in an emergency? Clearly, the governor's council would have supported a decision to allow the ships to leave with the tea in their holds.

Governor Hutchinson must have realized the patriots would not allow the tea to be landed and the tax paid. After all, they had stationed guards on each of the three ships. The governor also knew what members of his governor's council thought about landing the tea. The Boston consignees (factors) of East India

Company tea, including two of the governor's sons, petitioned the governor, seeking to have the Massachusetts government assume responsibility for unloading and storing the tea until new instructions regarding its disposal could be secured from the company. At that point, Governor Hutchinson called his council into session to advise him. Council members met first on November 19 but, not reaching a firm conclusion, adjourned until November 23. Again, they declined to make a judgment on the tea consignees' petition and adjourned until Saturday, November 27. At that point, a three-member committee received the task of writing a policy statement in response to the petition. When the council again met on Monday, November 29, the members considered and unanimously approved the committee's document. In it, the issue of parliamentary taxation on the colonies was reviewed and condemned. The Tea Act came in for two criticisms:

> This Act, in a commercial view, they [the council] think introductive of monopolies, and tending to bring on them the extensive evils thence arising. But their great objection to it is from its being manifestly intended...to secure the payment of the duty on the tea...which deprives the colonists of the right above mentioned [to tax themselves through their representatives] which they hold to be so essential a one that it cannot be taken away or given up....

Following this, the council addressed the tea consignees' petition to have the government take control of the tea when it arrived. Surprise, surprise, councilors unequivocally rejected that request, noting that "the duty on the tea becomes payable, and must be paid or secured to be paid on its being landed...."This, the council argued would be: "inconsistent with the declared sentiment of both houses in the last winter session of the General Court [Massachusetts legislature]...." So, though the governor's council did not explicitly recommend having the tea returned to London, members did express clearly their view that the tea should not be landed, for to approve the landing would imply approval of paying the tea tax.[121]

Wouldn't Hutchinson have been justified in granting waivers to laws and regulations requiring the tea's removal from the ships in order to protect East India Company property? The king may have thought so, for he saw fit to replace Hutchinson as governor after learning of the tea party and the governor's inaction.

A few months later, King George III approved the appointment of an "interim" Governor of the Massachusetts Bay Colony so that Thomas Hutchinson could travel to London for consultation—a polite way of ending Hutchinson's tenure as governor. Certainly, King George reasoned, making a Lieutenant General in the British Army the governor of Massachusetts Bay would bring Boston's rabble under control while holding the rest of the colony in check.

Before a change in governors was effected, a second "tea party" occurred in Boston. On March 7, 1774, patriots found that the recently docked brig Fortune had twenty-eight and one-half chests of tea in its hold. "Indians," whether painted or pale-faced, went on board that evening and offered a reprise of the show held on December 16, 1773. In this case, though, the East India Company suffered no loss, for the tea had been purchased privately in London.[122]

The second event created little stir in Boston, but in London, Lord North used it to show that Bostonians had no remorse for the earlier destruction of private property. The second event also demonstrated that the patriots were both determined and vigilant. Further, given that the "Indians" acted on the day the captain registered the ship's cargo with the customs office rather than waiting until the day before the grace period expired, people's anger against the tea tax was made manifest. Local patriots did not wait for "authority" from local committees of correspondence to dump the tea. Instead, they took "authority" into their own hands.[123]

But back to the matter of East India Company tea.

Boston wasn't the only East India Company tea destination. In fact the company secured an export license for the shipment of

600,000 pounds of tea to America. In addition to Boston, major consignments were directed to Philadelphia, New York City, and Charleston. Yet despite vigorous opposition to the tea shipments, in none of those cities was a "tea party" held to destroy East India Company tea.[124]

Curiously, Philadelphia's patriots led the way in opposing the landing—and taxing—of tea. The "curiosity" is that in previous episodes of colonial opposition to British tax policies, Philadelphia's patriots followed while others led.

The first formal colonial protest against the East India Company plan arose in Philadelphia on October 16, 1773. A mass meeting on that date which local patriot leaders promoted, and weighted heavily toward skilled artisans, mechanics (meaning journeymen craftsmen and small shopkeepers), and others of the middle class, formulated and passed a series of resolutions attacking the tea-tax plan. They demanded that merchants selected to receive and market the tea resign their appointments, and sent copies of the resolutions to other cities in the American colonies. In fact, patriot groups in several major cities, starting with Boston, soon adopted these resolutions or used them as the basis for promulgating their own.[125]

Despite this initial success, patriot leaders did not have an easy time in Philadelphia. As proved the case later in New York City and Charleston, various factions vied for domination of Philadelphia's approach to handling tea and tax issues. Most particularly, some conservative Quaker merchants denigrated the Patriot Society, which a number of Philadelphia's artisans and mechanics had organized the previous year. All the while, other local merchants favored a plan to resist the tea act. Patriot Society members persevered, demonstrated their unity and strength, and with the support of some merchants and professional men, led the fight against landing the tea.

A committee appointed at the October 16 meeting went to tea consignees and demanded they resign their appointment as East

India Company agents. At first, the merchants issued ambiguous responses to the demand. Committee members persisted.

Apparently aware that a large body of people, mostly mechanics and men of similar standing, but also including a number of prominent citizens, was backing the committee, and perhaps fearful of what fate might befall them if they defied the patriots, one after another agent caved in and resigned the appointment. Thomas Wharton led the list of resignations. He was a prosperous tea merchant who previously had been in the forefront of those criticizing the Patriot Society for its stand against the tea tax. Still, the give-and-take between some tea consignees and the committee did not end until the consignees received formal notice from Britain that when they took possession of the tea they would have to pay the Townshend three-pence-per-pound duty on it. With that confirmed, the last holdouts signed a resignation note on December 2.

Having their first goal in hand, patriot leaders now worked to keep the tea ship away from the customs zone and force the captain to return to England. Soon, handbills appeared around the docks announcing that any Delaware River pilot who guided a tea ship into Philadelphia would be facing an unpleasant bath of warm tar and goose feathers. The same fate was promised the captain who brought a tea ship into port.[126]

Waiting nervously for the arrival of the good ship Polly (a much larger vessel than any of the three which docked in Boston), on which were 598 East India Company tea chests, patriots kept up their supporters' spirits by printing letters in Philadelphia's newspapers. Then, like manna from heaven, on December 24 came word from Boston reporting the Tea Party! This was followed with news that the Polly had been spotted.[127]

The Polly's captain must have realized something was up when he could not persuade any of the pilot boats to guide the Polly up the river. He decided to labor on without help and ease his way into Philadelphia.

A large crowd gathered at a point below the city that overlooked the river. Seeing he was being summoned, the captain anchored his ship and rowed ashore. He was taken into town where he stood before a crowd estimated at 8,000 people, a crowd so large it had to meet outside, in the square before the State House. The large crowd (representing about a quarter of Philadelphia's population), plus statements the tea consignees made that they would not accept the tea, convinced the captain he should not attempt to land his ship at Philadelphia, but rather return it to England with his entire cargo.

According to a report written a few days later: "The whole business was conducted with a decorum and order worthy of the importance of the cause."

After it was re-supplied for the voyage, the Polly turned east and headed for England on December 28. Philadelphia's patriots had achieved their two goals: preventing the East India Company tea from being landed, and avoiding violence.[128]

New York had the earliest warning concerning the East India Company-British Government plan for selling duties tea in the colonies. The New York Mercury printed Parliament's Tea Act in its September 6 edition. Even so, patriot leaders had a much harder time than either Boston's or Philadelphia's patriots in uniting the various factions. Complicating the patriots' effort was deep-seated political animosity between two factions. They had been vying for dominance within the provincial legislature for many years.

The De Lancey and Livingston factions were not monoliths. While the De Lancey group was led by aristocrats and tended to be pro-government, and the Livingstons challenged both the Governor and Parliament, each included elements of varying social and economic standings, and of differing sentiments. Further complicating the negotiations were the varied merchants' views, including those actively engaged in smuggling Dutch tea into the colonies and others who more-or-less made their living through legitimate trade. Then there were the mechanics' views, both skilled artisans and retail tradesmen.[129]

Patriot leaders got the jump on other factions by calling a meeting in the city in mid-October. This led to a series of conferences, a rash of newspaper arguments, and sessions between the governor and his council, which the De Lancey faction dominated.

Following a second city meeting in late November, a committee visited merchants who were to receive consignments from the East India Company. All consignees agreed not to sell dutied tea. For a short time Governor Tyron thought that though the consignees would not pay the duty on the tea, he would be able to have the tea landed and placed in government storage.

Boston sent word to New York that it had resolved to have the tea returned to England on the ships in which it arrived. This notification worked like a ramrod in the spine of New York's Sons of Liberty. They pledged to follow Boston's lead, if the governor did not interfere.

Governor Tyron was determined not to make the same mistake he had when, as Governor of North Carolina in 1771, he put down a protest on the western frontier with armed force. At that time the Carolina frontiersmen had labeled him a tyrant. This time he was determined the government would not flex its muscle. The governor announced he wanted the tea landed, but would not use force to do so. And there the situation remained until word arrived of the Boston Tea Party. With that story flashing across the pages of New York newspapers, those who had hoped there might be a chance of landing the tea and storing it in one of the army barracks accepted defeat.

Pledges to see that the tea was returned to England could only be carried into effect when a tea ship arrived at New York's shores. For that, patriots and government men alike had a long wait. The large tea ship Nancy left England in mid-November, but labored in its passage, and was slow arriving off the American coast. Before it could reach New York, a heavy storm assaulted and damaged it. The captain found himself well off course and in need of repairs. He reached Antigua, where, while repairs were under way, he learned the fate of tea ships sent to Boston and Philadelphia. Still, he had his orders, so he resumed his voyage to New York.

The Nancy dropped its anchor near Sandy Hook on April 18, 1774, having survived yet another heavy storm with additional damage to its superstructure. A large crowd, including the tea consignees, met the captain when he came ashore. Upon learning the consignees would not accept the tea or pay the duty, the captain recognized he had little choice but to reprovision his ship and return to England. Five days later, the captain took a pilot boat out to his ship, and the following day the Nancy was again plying Atlantic waves, this time heading for England.[130]

Yet the "tea story" for New York was not quite over. While the Nancy episode was playing out, another ship, the London, carrying mixed cargo, came into New York's port.

Unbeknownst to the ship's owner, the captain had spirited a cargo of eighteen boxes of privately purchased tea on board. The captain did not know that another ship previously had landed in Philadelphia and reported the tea consignment on the London to the patriots. Philadelphia's Committee of Correspondence forwarded the information to its counterpart in New York.

At first the captain denied he had any tea on board. But New York patriots eventually persuaded the captain to admit the truth of the report Philadelphia patriots had sent them. This placed the ship's owner in a vulnerable position. If he tried to have the tea unloaded and the tax paid, he would face the wrath of the patriots; if he did not unload it and could not obtain customs papers clearing the ship to return to England, when the twenty-day grace period ended for paying duty, the customs officers could confiscate the tea. That the owner did not know the ship was carrying a consignment of tea was no defense as far as the customs agents were concerned.

Patriots called another mass meeting and explained various alternatives to the crowd of thousands. Likely through a prearranged plan, "Mohawks" went on board the ship, hauled out the boxes, and dumped the tea into the harbor. Then they took the boxes to the street in front of Merchant's Coffee House, and started a celebration bonfire. Because the tea actually had been purchased in London, and therefore was not part of the East India Company consignment, Parliament did not scrutinize New York's tea party.[131]

Further south, Charleston already had been the scene of a peaceful confrontation over tea. News of the tea act came late to the city, and word of a ship carrying tea to Charleston even later. Patriot leaders had little time to organize their opposition. They also were in the weakest position of all four urban patriot groups. They somehow had to bring together the disparate attitudes and values of three very different economic and social groups.

South Carolina was a colony where production agriculture held sway. Particularly important were the plantation owners who produced rice and indigo. The British allowed rice to be exported to southern Europe without first stopping in London, and offered a bounty on indigo sent to England. Those planters, who valued the export permits and bounties they received from England, were influential among all the elite in the colony. Another potent group, of course, was the merchants, some of whom considered rice and indigo planters to be their most important clients. Finally, there were the Charleston mechanics and tradesmen. Though they were not as ill treated by the upper class as their counterparts in Philadelphia, realistically they had limited economic or political influence. What they may have lacked in influence they made up for in part through sheer numbers.

One help the patriots had was the outspoken support two newspaper publishers provided. Both republished strong rebukes of the tea act from northern newspapers. They also brought in locally written letters condemning the scheme. Yet the patriots had not marshaled unified support in opposition to the tea shipment when a ship arrived on December 2 with 257 chests of tea on board. Before the patriots could take action, the captain entered his list of cargo, including the tea, into the custom's office records. The tea, though, remained on board his ship.[132]

Calling a meeting to discuss the situation, patriot leaders secured a pledge from the two merchant firms to which the tea had been consigned that they would not accept the cargo, and would not pay the duty on the tea. Serious disagreements between planters and merchants left the meeting's leaders without an action plan. The governor chose to wait out the situation.

As the twenty day grace period neared an end, patriots attempted to intimidate the captain into returning it to England. The captain succeeded in calling their bluff, but he won a hollow victory. When the grace period ended, customs officers unloaded the tea and stored it in a government warehouse, leaving the captain without compensation for shipping the tea across the Atlantic.

The East India Company sent a message to the governor of South Carolina in the spring of 1774, demanding that he sell the tea (presumably after paying the duty on it). He ignored the message. The tax never was paid on the tea stored in Charleston, and a year or so later, the revolutionary government of South Carolina sold the untaxed tea to raise money in support of its war for independence from Britain.[133]

This accounts for all but one of the ships carrying East India Company tea to America. That ship, the William (which Jonathan Clarke owned: a relative through marriage to Thomas Hutchinson, Jr., and one of the tea consignees), was destined for Boston, but encountered a storm and, on December 10, 1773, was blown ashore on Cape Cod. Clarke learned of this and galloped to Provincetown. There he oversaw the landing of fifty-eight chests of tea, and, with Governor Hutchinson's personal approval, had all but two of the chests taken to Castle William. One of the remaining two went to a Provincetown merchant to sell, but local patriots learned of this and destroyed the tea. The other reached the village of Wellfleet, where some tea actually was sold before local patriots took charge of the remainder. They destroyed it. Just what happened to the tea taken to Castle William has never been discovered, but none of the Massachusetts customs offices left records of receiving tax payment for any of the tea.[134]

Some other events involving local patriot groups and tea merchants occurred in several colonies. The most notable of these was in Annapolis, Maryland. In early October 1774, almost ten months after the Boston Tea Party, the brig Peggy Stewart docked there with a mixed cargo. One of the ship's owners, Anthony Stewart, first tried to register the cargo, other than 2,000 pounds of privately purchased tea. A customs officer refused his request. Stewart entered the tea and paid the duty on it. Members of a local committee of observation called a mass meeting to consider Stewart's action. That gathering determined that the tea should not be landed, and appointed a small committee to see that all the cargo other than the tea was unloaded. Another meeting the following day determined that an apology from Stewart as well as the tea consignees, along with a public burning of the tea would be sufficient to end the matter. Unfortunately for Stewart, a small, vocal minority demanded that the ship be burned. The crowd overwhelmingly rejected this demand, but Stewart was concerned for his wife, who was on the verge of having a baby. He thought the extremists might attack his house, and he feared for his wife and child. Stewart and the tea consignees went on board the ship, lifted the tea to the deck, raised the ship's flags, and unfurled the sails. Then he set the tea and the brig on fire. It burned to the water line.[135]

In the spring of 1773, East India Company officials gleefully looked forward to dumping 600,000 pounds of tea on American shores for a handsome profit, and Parliament anticipated seeing a long-standing tea tax finally generating both a sizable sum and a firm precedent for levying future taxes on the colonies. But by the spring of 1774, when the various governors reported the situation in their respective colonies, optimism turned to a mix of bewilderment and acute anger. Over two thirds of the East India tea was returned to London warehouses, but the company owed shipping costs in excess of 2,100 pounds sterling for its trip to America and back to London. The remainder had disappeared, without any income flowing to the company. For the Government, its power to tax the colonies again had been denied, and its authority flaunted.

But why had Charleston, Philadelphia, and New York patriots managed to hold their own against both the East India Company and the British Government without resorting to violence, while Boston's patriots rejected any compromise and risked the city's fate by destroying some 9,000 pounds sterling worth of private property? Many asked this question at the time. It has been explored by historians since.

In background summary: Following the end of the French and Indian War in 1763, whenever an intercolonial conflict arose with Britain, Boston's patriots led the way.

In 1765, when news of the Stamp Act reached the colonies, Boston's mob took out after Andrew Oliver, recently appointed stamp distributor for Massachusetts Bay. Though Oliver escaped the mob, his office was destroyed, and his home damaged. Oliver resigned his stamp distributor's appointment the next day.[136]

After Parliament canceled the Stamp Act, it next tried to raise revenue in the colonies through the Townshend Act, passed in 1768. That Act imposed taxes on glass, lead, painter's colors, paper, and tea. Again, with Boston strongly supporting resistance, American colonies united in a boycott of British goods. Parliament eventually responded in 1770 by dropping all the duties except the three-pence-per-pound tax on tea.[137]

Boston then sent mixed messages to its fellow colonists. First, its patriots advocated maintaining the boycott until Parliament lifted the tea tax. Merchants in Boston, New York, and elsewhere protested they had lost enough business through two years of boycotts and refused to support its continuance. All people had to do, the merchants argued, was to not buy duued tea. The Boston patriots stamped their collective foot and demanded the boycott continue, but without admitting this to their compatriots to the south, they did nothing to persuade Boston merchants to maintain the boycott.

Meanwhile, New York and Philadelphia tea merchants were smuggling Dutch tea into their markets. In fact, in 1772, New Yorkers paid the British duty on 530 pounds of tea instead of the 320,000 pounds of English tea they had imported the year before the Townshend Duties went into effect. The drop in imported English tea to Philadelphia was equally dramatic: from 175,000 pounds in 1768 to a paltry 128 pounds in 1772. But, as a customs agent in Boston reported to a pro-government newspaper there, Boston merchants imported about as much taxed tea in 1771 as they had before the tax was imposed: some 265,000 pounds. Furthermore, shipping magnet John Hancock, a vigorous supporter of the patriot cause, was paid freight on transporting more than 40,000 pounds of taxed tea. When New York and Philadelphia newspapers published stories about Boston's love affair with taxed tea, Boston's patriots came in for a storm of criticism.[138]

If Boston's patriots were not steadfast in resisting the shipment and sale of taxed tea in 1773, they could give up any hope of returning to the forefront of American patriot activity.

Heightening the Bostonians' dilemma was their pledge in the fall of 1773, grandly communicated to their compatriots in New York and elsewhere, that they were determined to secure the resignations of the tea consignees in their city, and then to see the tea returned to England without having the tax paid. Indeed their unequivocal statements to this effect had galvanized New York's patriots to pursue the same tactics.

On the morning of November 3, 1773, posters appeared around Boston announcing a noon meeting by the Liberty Tree at which time the tea consignees were to resign their commissions. Noon came, and with it a large crowd. Missing were the tea merchants. The crowd appointed a committee and charged it with obtaining the merchants' resignations. Committee members failed to accomplish their mission. With this failure, the patriots could not possibly allow the tea to be landed and still have any credibility with patriots throughout Massachusetts or elsewhere.

Governor Hutchinson may have offered to have the tea unloaded to Castle William with a pledge to hold it there until information could be secured from East India Company officials in London as to its disposition. That hardly was a realistic offer for the patriots to accept, since two of the governor's sons were consignees, and a third consignee was a son-in-law. All three of them had ready access to Castle William and could spirit away cartons of tea any time they were sure patriots were not in a position to catch them. Therefore, December 16 was the patriots' last chance to show everyone—Governor Hutchinson, hesitant patriots in inland Massachusetts towns, and skeptical patriots to the south—that Bostonians were determined not to purchase taxed tea. Had they failed to act on that date, on December 17, customs officers no doubt would have gone onto the Dartmouth and confiscated its tea chests, after which the consignees would have paid the duty on it and put the tea up for sale in their stores. The same would have happened when the other two vessels' twenty-day waiting period expired.

Careful plans for dumping the tea into the harbor seem to have been laid well in advance. Just when and by whom can only be speculated. Several of Boston's leading patriots belonged to the Loyal Nine Club, the North End Caucus, or to the Long Room Club. Skilled artisans and small storeowners dominated these local social clubs, but some club memberships also included several of the most prominent men in the city. Now the clubs seconded as patriot organizations. Other patriots were active in Boston's Grand Lodge of Masons. In fact, the Masons had a scheduled meeting on the evening of December 16, but canceled it because most members failed to attend. A coalition of these groups could have met secretly with the existing Sons of Liberty organization before December 16, and worked out details for destroying the tea. More likely, however, an all-day meeting of representatives from committees of correspondence of Boston and several neighboring towns was where tea party plans were developed and approved. Some members of the North End Caucus, the Long Room Club, and the Masons also held membership in Boston's Committee of Correspondence.

By including representatives from inland committees of correspondence in the planning, Boston's patriots would have shown they were not acting alone, but in concert with their "country" brethren. Such a meeting was, in fact, held on December 13 at Faneuil Hall.[139]

Now that Bostonians had destroyed private property of considerable value, the question arose both in England and America, how would the British government respond? Was John Adams right when he asked the rhetorical question: "Will they punish us?"

VI

Parliament Decides It's Time
to Teach Those Treasonous
Colonists a Lesson

First came American colonists' negative reactions and ideological rejections to Parliament's postwar efforts to raise tax revenue in those colonies. Then there were the dramatic—climactic—Boston Tea Party, along with the less dramatic, but equally firm rejections of East India Company's taxed tea shipments to Charleston and Philadelphia (the New York story was still to come).

Now it is time to consider how Lord North's administration and Parliament responded to America's rejections of the tea shipments.

Prime Minister Lord North, and Secretary for the American Department, Lord Dartmouth, had backed the East India Company's tea export plan with their eyes open. They did so knowing the Americans might not welcome taxed tea shipped to them through a new monopolistic marketing plan. Both men had witnessed American opposition to the Stamp Act in 1765, and to the Townshend Duties in 1768. Each time, Parliament had devised a "compromise" of sorts and Americans had returned to normal commercial relations with their mother country.

Both Prime Minister North and Lord Dartmouth were well acquainted with other conflicts that had developed between individual colonial legislatures and British government policies. These included government prohibition of colonial issuance of paper currency as legal tender, and government demand that colonies construct barracks to house British troops stationed in their midst, against the colonial legislators' opposition. There was continuing aggravation between colonial legislatures which wanted to extend representation to newly settled areas in the west of their colonies and British administrators. London said despite growing populations, colonial legislatures did not have authority to increase the number of members in the lower house, thus depriving representation in the legislature of the ever-expanding western settlements.[140]

Both North and Dartmouth must have known that while New England and the South had resumed the purchase of taxed tea in 1770, after ending the boycott on British goods in protest of the Townshend Duties, the middle colonies had opted to continue purchasing smuggled tea from Holland. Perhaps Boston and Charleston would welcome the now cheap English tea, which continued to be taxed, and the real test would be in either Philadelphia or New York.

The two men were unlikely to have forgotten the comment Britain's North American Commander of the Navy made in mid-1773, when he wrote from his station in Boston: "British Acts of Parliament will never go down in America, unless forced by the point of a sword." Neither would they have forgotten about the British customs sloop Gaspee going aground in June 1772 near Warwick, Rhode Island. The sloop's captain was notorious for confiscating local farmers' animals for food and cutting down productive fruit trees for firewood. Upon learning of the grounding, a prosperous Providence merchant led a group of local men on board, wounded the captain, sent the crew packing, and burned the sloop to the waterline. Nor would the parliamentary leaders have forgotten that when the British government ordered a Court of Inquiry, members of the Court could find no credible person who would admit knowing the name of any of those Rhode

Islanders involved in the attack, though those boarding the Gaspee wore no disguises.

Finally, there was a frantic letter Governor Hutchinson sent his superiors in London, warning that the patriots were publishing documents which were "tending to sedition and mutiny, and some of them expressly denying parliamentary authority."[141]

No doubt some in Lord North's cabinet must have wondered why Governor Hutchinson spoke of the patriots' mutinous actions, but did nothing to counter them, other than to move the Massachusetts legislative sessions four miles outside of Boston, to Cambridge. Hutchinson was, after all, the Massachusetts Colony's chief executive. Others may well have thought that Hutchinson was simply overreacting to spirited writing, for which patriots seemed to have a penchant.

Yet, those patriots who participated in the Boston Tea Party were so audacious and their destruction of boatloads of tea so extreme, they shocked the prime minister and his cabinet officer for America.

Lord Dartmouth, who was Lord North's stepbrother, had taken his post as American secretary in 1772. He had a reputation for being sympathetic toward the colonies when he was President of the Board of Trade, but his principal allegiance was to his half-brother as well as the king, not to America. Even so, as the person responsible for fashioning a response to Boston, he sought to minimize the damage the government inflicted on that blighted colony while still upholding British authority.

Keeping the response out of parliamentary politics seems to have been foremost in Dartmouth's mind. If the cabinet could be seen meting out appropriate punishment through swift, decisive action, public anger could be calmed, and cool heads in Parliament could be lined up to counter those who would be out for total dominance of the colony. Also, by focusing on Boston, rejection of the tea in Philadelphia and its being stored without being sold in Charleston might be ignored. (At the time Dartmouth was pondering Boston's fate no East India Company tea had yet arrived in New York, but Governor Tyron's letters indicated he would be powerless to force its unloading. Still, hope remained that no violence would occur there.)

Lord Dartmouth quickly collected the names of those in London who had been in Boston at the time the Tea Party took place. He had the men make sworn statements regarding the event and the meetings preceding it. He also secured the names of those most prominent in the meetings. All the while, he was pressing the Attorney General's office for a ruling as to whether the meetings and the Tea Party itself constituted "High Treason" within the laws of the empire.[142]

A determination came back from the Attorney General that, based on the information Dartmouth had supplied regarding the meetings and their probable connection to the Tea Party, and, certainly the party itself, constituted high treason. There remained the matter of evidence against alleged perpetrators.

Some dozen witnesses in London who had been in Boston on the fateful day prepared depositions as to what they saw. These went to both the Attorney General and Solicitor General for review. If the length of time they took before responding indicates the care they gave in reviewing the statements, they were thorough, indeed, for there was a nine day lapse between the statements' submission and responses to the cabinet, even though it was clear this was a matter of greatest urgency.

Dartmouth had to feel utterly deflated when, on the last day of February, both the Attorney General and the Solicitor General maintained that "the charge of High Treason cannot be maintained against any individuals on the ground of the depositions taken at the cabinet Board." All he could do about prosecuting individuals, then, would be to ask future Governor Gage, upon his arrival in Massachusetts, to take legal action against alleged leaders of the uprising. Even then Dartmouth felt compelled to issue a caution that if Gage felt a prosecution could not generate convictions due to popular resentment against Britain, "it would be better to desist from prosecution, seeing that an ineffectual attempt would only be triumph to the faction and disgraceful to Government."[143]

A second nonparliamentary action Dartmouth had envisioned was closing the Port of Boston to commercial trade. Commerce there would resume only when Bostonians provided restitution to the East India Company for the destroyed tea. He believed this could be handled by moving customs officers out of Boston to other Massachusetts ports. To make sure the cabinet had legal authority to do this on its own, he asked the Law Officers for an opinion well before a decision had been reached on the treason matter. On February 11, Dartmouth received the reply he had hoped for. The lawyers advised that the king's government "may appoint the custom houses in such ports of the province as in their discretion they think most convenient...."[144]

Following a tête-à-tête with the prime minister, Dartmouth prepared a directive to the Treasury Department to select a new port headquarters for customs officers. He sent this draft to North, only to have it returned with recommendations for changes. Lord North noted: "I think as it is to be entered among our papers, it had better relate only to the removal of the Custom House officers...." At the same time notice was drawn up to the North American Naval Commander to instruct his officers to be vigilant in not allowing any ships into Boston harbor that did not have customs commissioners' permission. Presumably, only ships carrying food or fuel would be allowed to dock in Boston. These communications were prepared more than a week before the cabinet learned Tea Party leaders could not be prosecuted effectively for treason.[145]

Despite the rapid-fire activity, some members of Parliament were impatient. Even before the cabinet reached tentative decisions on action against Tea Party leaders and the town of Boston, a powerful Member of Parliament announced he wanted the documents relating to the event placed before Parliament. Perhaps because the writer was both a hard-liner and a Lord North supporter, he was assured that the papers would be delivered in due course.[146]

On February 19, the cabinet voted to ask Parliament for legislation closing the Port, moving the Massachusetts government out of Boston, and significantly changing the Massachusetts form of government as outlined in the 1691 charter.

Why Lord North decided on this change from cabinet action against Boston to parliamentary legislation against both Boston and the colony of Massachusetts Bay has puzzled historians for centuries. No written communication between North and Dartmouth addressing this has been found, other than the note North sent Dartmouth regarding orders to the Treasury to move the Customs House out of Boston, as quoted above. The most likely explanation seems to be that Dartmouth's initial directive to the Treasury that North rejected may have indicated the move was to be temporary, until Boston paid for the destroyed tea. The Attorney General's interpretation did not address that, but rather: "Treasury may appoint the custom house in such ports of the province as in their discretion they think most convenient for the purpose." The prime minister may have decided that this language did not protect the cabinet if the customs office's move was based on the desire to punish Boston until the city paid for the destroyed tea. If North saw he or Dartmouth could be vulnerable to a charge of acting outside the law, then they had better have a parliamentary bill passed which made clear the customs office move was intended to force payment for the tea.

The decision to go to Parliament drastically altered the approach Lord North and Secretary Dartmouth had been developing in response to the Tea Party. In doing so, North caused a fundamental shift in the nature of the contest.[147]

As long as government action was being taken against alleged perpetrators and in an effort to secure redress for the East India Company's losses, the issues involved were narrow and related to law and equity. Residents of other colonies likely would feel resentment toward the British government for punishing all of Boston for actions "a few troublemakers" caused. They might even send food packages to help those unfortunate Bostonians who suffered from the port's closing. Their views toward the mother country were unlikely to change as a result of these actions, but once Parliament entered the fray, the gloves were off.

Members of Parliament, both Lord North's supporters and opponents, surely would make plain the fundamental issue the Tea Party raised was one of constitutionalism. They almost certainly would argue that the Parliament—king, lords, and commons acting as one body—was the sovereign power in the empire. Otherwise, the colonies were, in fact, alien states. Members of Parliament knew the answer to this presumed dilemma: Parliament was the supreme legislature not only for Britain, but also for the empire. There really was no dilemma, only a matter of teaching the colonists to accept their inferior status and the requirement that they submit to Parliament's will.

Given colonists' sweeping rejection of Parliament's Tea Act, from Boston to Charleston, cabinet ministers must have had some inkling they might be in for tough days ahead. With encouragement from those who should have known better, cabinet members entered the new phase of responses to the Tea Party expecting they would be able to enforce their will on the colonies without armies being involved, or blood being spilled.[148]

In early February 1774, King George interviewed General Gage as the candidate to replace Massachusetts Bay Governor Thomas Hutchinson. Gage, whose wife was American, had served in the colonies for twenty years before his relatively recent return to England. As a seasoned military man, his views commanded respect.

When the king asked General Gage about potential colonial resistance to British authority, Gage replied that the colonists "will be Lions, whilst we are Lambs, but if we take the resolute part they will undoubtedly prove very meek." He added that he would see Massachusetts put in an orderly manner without having to call for additional troops. If that were the case for the firebrands in Boston, then presumably colonial response to parliamentary policy, and action against Boston and Massachusetts, would not provoke a crisis in America.[149]

While Parliament was in the early phase of planning action against Boston, Massachusetts Governor Thomas Hutchinson was assessing the situation in that city. Even though a customs officer had been tarred and feathered, the second "tea party" had transpired, and the East India Company tea consignees so feared for their lives they remained in Castle William, Hutchinson wrote on March 21, 1774, that: "an opposition to His Majesty's forces is so wild and extravagant a design that I cannot bring myself to believe even the present leaders of the people so mad" as to plan an armed uprising. He then was specific, saying: "I have not been satisfied that there had yet been any such rebellious insurrections as would have justified…bringing forward the military power to suppress them."[150]

Britain's cabinet kept its legislative intentions secret until Lord North revealed to Parliament the first phase of its planned response to the Tea Party and other issues flowing from Massachusetts. Furthermore, on March 14, when North prepared to open debate on cabinet plans for the Port of Boston, he had the galleries cleared so the debate would be held in secret. Then he outlined his legislative intent: to close the Port and move customs officers to other Massachusetts ports. In response to a question, he refused to identify any port to which customs agents might be assigned. He did say the agents would be returned to Boston only after the East India Company had been compensated for the lost tea and citizens had demonstrated their willingness to treat government officials properly. He also noted that the proposed legislation was to be followed by measures designed to address other problems in the administration of government in Massachusetts Bay.[151]

Lord North next elevated the level of confrontation between Massachusetts and Parliament, clearly stating the fundamental issue was not over the tea tax: "we are now to dispute the question whether we have or have not any authority in that country." In short, the problem was not one of attempting to punish a few violent men and persuading citizens of Boston to show proper respect to Crown officials. The problem was one of constitutional interpretation. Did Parliament have supreme authority over all the empire, or were the colonies tied to Britain only by their allegiance to the monarchy? Thus, the prime minister completely abandoned the initial plan to focus narrowly on Boston's destruction of private property in violation of the law.[152]

Debate moved forward in the Commons through three readings of the Boston Port Act, with some criticism and significant support in the debate, but no opposition in its passage. One interesting observation came from the youngest member of the Commons. In his early twenties, the Member of Commons wondered if his generation was to be saddled with the heavy debt remaining from the Seven Years War without reaping any benefits that the war presumably had brought to the British Empire.[153]

Next came debate in the House of Lords. The speed with which the cabinet wished to see the bill passed prompted the Lords to meet on a Saturday to hear its first reading. Not until the second reading on Monday was there any debate. It made clear that cabinet members, of whom most held seats in the House of Lords, supported the Boston Port Bill, but were not in agreement that it provided appropriate punishment for recalcitrant colonists in that city. Further, a member of the Lords, though not a cabinet member but a close confidant of King George III, applauded the Tea Party as providing the government an opportunity of passing legislation which would show that it was no longer treating the colonists with kid gloves, but "that we should temporize no longer." With such legislation in place, he implied that British authority would be reestablished in America.[154]

The bill had its third reading the following day and was forwarded to the king who signed it on March 31. The first of what was to be four "coercive acts," from the British viewpoint, and five "intolerable acts" from the colonists' standpoint was ready for implementation on June 1, the effective date given in the act for closing the Port of Boston. Lord North must have been pleased that not only had he secured passage of the bill with minimum objections, but that he had done so within the time frame he had set: before the Easter recess.[155]

The Port Bill was to generate strong reactions beyond Boston and Massachusetts Bay. But criticism of it came mostly from other port cities and towns. The next legislation the North government introduced in Parliament involved threats to all American colonists, whether they lived in ports, inland towns, rural communities, or were in hinterland cabins. This was the Massachusetts Government Act.

Cabinet members looked upon the bill as "remedial" rather than "coercive." The problem it addressed from their perspective was the colony's excessively democratic government as outlined in its 1691 charter.

First, a brief description of the government in a royal colony, as differentiated from a proprietary colony (such as Maryland or Pennsylvania), in which a citizen of Britain "owned" the colony, or a charter colony, which placed the government in the colonial citizens' hands. (Connecticut and Rhode Island were charter colonies, as, indeed, had been Massachusetts Bay before 1684, when it became a royal colony.)

A colonial government with a royal charter operated under the king's direct authority (actually administered by the king's officials). A royal colony had legislative, executive, and judicial bodies, though they were not necessarily independent of each other. The legislative body included a lower and an upper house. While the governor commanded executive authority, he operated with the advice and, often, consent of the governor's council, which was identical to the upper house of the legislature. So, the same men acted as legislators while sitting as the upper house, and as members of the executive, when they acted as the governor's council. The judiciary included a colony-wide superior court and lower courts, most commonly operating at the county level and often judged by several county justices of the peace. Then there were county sheriffs and lesser enforcement and administrative officers. County and town governments varied by region, but in Massachusetts the dominant local government unit was the town meeting at which all taxpayers in the township had equal voice. Town meetings could be held whenever an issue justified calling the taxpayers together.

In all royal governments freeholders (property taxpayers) elected members to the lower house, according to county and township districts. In all royal colonies other than Massachusetts Bay, royal authority in London chose the men to serve in the upper house/governor's council. Crown officials selected men of stature and influence in a colony, men who had demonstrated a willingness to support Royal priorities.

In Massachusetts Bay, the 1691 charter, granted shortly after the Glorious Revolution (which removed James II from the throne and country, and replaced him with William and Mary), decreed that members of the upper house were to be nominated annually by the lower house and the outgoing upper house meeting jointly, with the governor given veto power over individual appointments. In the judicial category, the Massachusetts members of the superior court, along with sheriffs and justices of the peace received appointment from the governor who made them with the advice and consent of his council. County grand juries were elected from a roster of town selectmen. In other royal colonies, the governor appointed all these judicial officers, and sheriffs chose jurors.

Town meetings were common in New England colonies, but did not exist in colonies to the south, where justices of the peace sat in county administrative courts.

Governors had some discretion to act without consulting their council, but on significant policy or administrative matters, they were expected to be guided by the council. This worked reasonably well in Massachusetts Bay up to the time of the Stamp Act, when the lower house saw an opportunity to force the governor's hand by giving him a council closely aligned with lower house members' views and in opposition to the Crown. From that time forward, the legislature nominated "men of substance" but excluded from the council those who were inclined to support undesirable parliamentary policies.

Both Governor Francis Bernard and his successor, Thomas Hutchinson, complained bitterly to London about the difficulty they had in carrying out unpopular Royal policies due to the council's opposition. Except in rare cases, other royal governors had no such problems.

Under the draft Massachusetts Government Act, Lord North asked Parliament to alter the Massachusetts Bay charter in order to change the selection process for certain officers. This was on its face a radical bill. Never before had the British government's legislative arm overturned a royal charter that the king had granted to a colony. Despite this, members of Parliament studied the bill without outward qualms.[156]

First, Lord North's bill mandated that the Crown would nominate members of the governor's council/upper house. The governor received specific authority to act on his own in emergency situations. The general nature of this article gave the Massachusetts governor more freedom of action than any other colonial governor. Next, the Crown would select superior court judges, and the governor would pick sheriffs and justices without having to confer with his council. Initially, North apparently feared to call for a new procedure for choosing grand juries, but during debate on the bill changed his mind and wrote into it authority for sheriffs to select grand juries. (The governor was to select county sheriffs.) Finally, because Governor Hutchinson had complained that town meetings, especially in Boston, had become too political, Lord North proposed to restrict them to one meeting per year with its agenda limited to the appointment of town selectmen (a body which administered township business when the town meeting was not sitting) and selection of men to represent the township in the colonial legislature's lower house. A provision allowed the governor to authorize additional town meetings upon petition.[157]

Unlike the Boston Port Bill, Lord North wanted members of Parliament to have time to think about the Massachusetts

Government Bill's provisions, and therefore introduced it shortly before the Easter recess. He also agreed that visitors would be allowed to watch the debates.

Following Parliament's Easter break, the bill moved forward in the Commons while the cabinet drafted yet another Massachusetts bill. Called the Massachusetts Justice Bill, it authorized the governor to move trials of government officials out of the colony if those officials were charged with a capital offense for actions they took in their official capacity. The bill was to have a three-year duration. It was introduced to the Commons before a final vote had been taken on the Massachusetts Government bill.[158]

Though the government's opponents in the Commons had several able debaters, they realized the public generally supported the government's position. To minimize potential damage to themselves, the opposition proposed a general debate on the combined bills, which would shorten the time devoted to them. Since the government had a very safe majority, and since it, too, wished to get along with business, North planned accordingly.

For a week at the end of April the two sides argued and bickered, often over minor points. Before they could agree to finalize the two pieces of legislation, the Secretary at War threw in yet another bill: the Quartering Act. Maintaining that four regiments were heading for Massachusetts Bay, and that the only barracks available were on an island in Boston harbor, he proposed to give the governor authority to commander taverns and empty buildings for troop housing.

Since Lord North and his colleagues made many changes in the Justice Bill during committee meetings, a member of the opposition asked to have it printed in its final form so all members would know on what they were voting. He asked in vain. A final vote was ordered without members being allowed to study its contents. They would find out on what they had voted after it was passed and printed. With that little matter out of the way, all three bills quickly were approved and sent to the House of Lords for their concurrence.[159]

Debate in the Lords generated little public interest, and proceeded without opposition lords making any bombastic contributions. After all, Lord North had been winning his point by majorities of over four to one. A leading opponent who had been absent due to sickness did drag himself to the Lords, and expostulated for over an hour. While the debate supposedly was over the Quartering Bill, he managed to condemn both the Port Act and the Massachusetts Government Act while indicating his support for parliamentary supremacy over the colonies. This time the administration garnered a smaller majority because many of the Lords were absent. The vote was fifty-seven for the government, sixteen against. Once the king signed his approval, what became known in the British press as the coercive acts became law. A short time later a rash of directives went from cabinet officers to Governor Gage.

When the colonists looked at the parliamentary legislation passed in the spring of 1774, they named them the Intolerable Acts, and they listed five, not four.[160]

Poor Prime Minister North! Here he was, laboring over ways to meet the king's demand that the American colonies be forced into "submission" without creating unnecessary bloodshed. And what did he do? In the midst of this he brought into play an issue with which all his predecessors back to Lord Bute, author of the Treaty of Paris in 1763, had struggled. Each of those prime ministers ultimately had punted it on to the next administration. Yet despite the crises he confronted with the Americans, Lord North decided to hold onto the ball and run it straight into the line.

The "ball" was Canada, or more specifically the province of Quebec. It was a land almost completely populated by French Catholic colonists.

Britain and France had been enemies for centuries, and British law had banned the practice of the Catholic faith since Elizabethan times. These factors promised many difficult decisions for any British government proposing to create an effective Quebec governing system.

From a political perspective the government chose perhaps the worst possible time to propose a bill it had been working on for years. Known commonly as the Quebec Act, the legislation was designed to bring order to the area French settlers had dominated for over a century.

Because the North government was the first stable administration in England since the war ended in 1763, it was able to come to grips with several sticky issues. The Province of Quebec extended down the St. Lawrence River from west of Montreal to the river's mouth, leaving the region around Lakes Ontario and Erie, and to the south with no formal government. Several British forts existed in that huge region, but for the most part, Indian tribes controlled it.

Quebec's residents overwhelmingly were of French heritage in culture, law, and language, and were members of the Roman Catholic faith. Indeed, under French law they were required to make annual payments to support the Church. Many Catholic priests worked among them. French law was in effect, and residents were regulated through an administrative government in which they had virtually no say.[161]

Once British officials assumed control of the Canadian government, they promoted English settlements. Yet a decade later, only a few hundred English speaking souls could be found in the Quebec province. The Church of England barely had a toehold. Catholic churches continued to thrive in the province, and French civil law applied to business and real estate transactions. A governor's council advised the chief executive, but no move had been made to create a legislative body. Then, too, the province's western boundary remained in question.

Some French settlers feared they could face forced removal, as had about six thousand French living in Acadia in 1755, when the governor of Nova Scotia sent them south, mostly to Louisiana's New Orleans area. And because England had laws banning the practice of the Catholic faith in that country, there was natural concern over their being allowed to practice their faith publicly.

By the time Lord North and his cabinet officers began work on a Quebec Bill in 1773, Quebec's population included fewer than one thousand English and over sixty-five thousand French. A review of the Treaty of Paris reminded government planners that England had pledged to respect the rights of those who practiced the Catholic faith, but hedged that pledge by adding: "as far as the laws of Great Britain admit." Since English law forbade the practice of Catholicism in the nation, a dilemma existed. The government also knew merely taking up the matter of establishing policies for administering Quebec was dangerous. In 1766, the sitting prime minister sought to regulate the laws applying to Quebec, and as a result of a conflict of opinion with the Lord Chancellor, King George III dismissed that prime minister. North was not ready to retire from government in 1773.

There also was the challenge of creating a legislature.[162]

The Proclamation of 1763, in seeking to promote English settlements, promised that the colonies recently acquired from France—Quebec and elsewhere—would have legislative assemblies. Presumably English settlers would control them, yet no step had been taken to create one in Quebec. Further, General Guy Carleton, Governor of Quebec, presented an argument against creating an elected legislature. He warned he did not have enough patronage plums to hand out to legislators in order to assure a majority of votes favorable to Crown policies—another dilemma.[163]

In late 1773 and early 1774, conflicting petitions came from Quebec's French and English communities. One area of agreement between them was a request to establish Quebec's western and southern boundary to include the eastern Great Lakes and the region to the south, down to the Ohio River. Such a change in borders would put the Crown government in direct conflict with colonial economic and political leaders in Virginia, Pennsylvania, and New York. They had invested heavily in speculative plans to develop parts of the Ohio Valley region for future settlements, and incorporation into their respective colonies.[164]

The Quebec Bill, which finally made its way out of the cabinet and to Parliament, was designed to bring order and stability to the government of Quebec, not necessarily to meet goals promised in the Treaty and subsequent Proclamation of 1763. Initially, it also took into account the expansionist aspirations and inland settlements political and economic leaders of the long-established Virginia, Pennsylvania, and New York colonies were advancing. The former matters—bringing order and stability to governing the French and English settlements in Quebec—were determined before the end of 1773. Those agreements also included the intention of not altering Quebec's western and southern borders, even though the government had received petitions from both English and French settlers seeking the province's expansion. Sometime after news of the Boston Tea Party arrived, the government added a section to the Bill, greatly expanding the border.[165]

Measures in the Quebec Bill that subsequently raised ire among American patriots involved the extension of Quebec's authority over the entire Ohio Valley. Coupled to this was the guarantee that French inhabitants were not subject to the Elizabethan oath of supremacy, and would be free to practice their Catholic faith. Compounding this was the presence of a Catholic Bishop in Quebec. Next was the issue of representative government. The Bill denied residents the right of an elected legislature. Instead, there was to be an appointed "legislative council" whose powers did not include levying taxes. Parliament kept that authority for itself. Some in the American colonies objected to other provisions, but these generated the greatest outrage. Indeed, Americans expressed far more anger than opposition members of Parliament showed during debates over the Bill.[166]

As a rare exception to protocol, the government first introduced the bill in the House of Lords, and directed that debate be held in secret. Even the London newspaper most adept in gaining information on secret debates failed to pierce the veil of secrecy.[167]

After the Lords passed the legislation and it moved to the Commons, one of the first challenges North faced was the fact the bill had been introduced in the Lords. Under parliamentary protocol, all money bills went first to the Commons, and the Quebec Bill called for levying tithes on residents for the support of the Catholic Church by French settlers and the Anglican Church by the English. North brushed aside this challenge, noting that when the cabinet had prepared the bill the Commons was deeply involved in debating the American legislation and this gave the Lords something to do while waiting to consider the American bills. Given the number of members the king and North controlled in the Commons, he had little to fear from opposition challenges, even one of such a sensitive nature.[168]

Opposition leaders attacked the Quebec Bill from several directions. The most serious involved the province's new boundaries. A leader of the Commons minority, who, on the side, represented the colony of New York in London, challenged the boundary extension into the Ohio Valley. He noted the western border of New York had not been set, and the projected Quebec boundary would impinge on New York's expansion. Others made similar claims for Pennsylvania and Virginia. Though promising that the boundary as proposed would not violate established colonial territorial lines, North was only willing to give way through inconsequential amendments. In the end, he argued that Crown commissioners would be called upon to arbitrate disputes. The bill finally passed the Commons with numerous amendments, was reintroduced into the Lords where its members approved the Commons amendments, and on June 22, 1774, the king signed it.

The Catholic toleration provisions in the Quebec Act caused King George III several minutes of distress as he made his formal procession to sign the bill on June 22. Some members of the watching crowd hurled taunts at him: "No Popery! No French laws!" This was merely a momentary petulant expostulation. When elections were held later in 1774, those candidates using the Quebec Act as a whipping post fared poorly.[169]

Parliament's reaction to the Tea Party began by reasserting parliamentary supremacy and demanding colonial subservience.

This came through the Boston Port Bill. Either Boston would pay for the destroyed tea and confess its error in dumping the tea into the harbor, or it would remain a port without a fleet. Indeed, after its passage, several small groups in both London and Boston sought to pay the damages. The government rejected their offers. Only a formal Boston municipal organization would be allowed to make the payment. Without that, and the apology, the port would remain closed.[170]

London journalists saw the Massachusetts Government Act as punitive in nature. Lords Dartmouth and North maintained it was simply designed to fix flaws in the 1691 Massachusetts Bay charter. Dartmouth said he had planned the previous year to bring forth a bill to replace the elected council members with Crown appointments, but was diverted by the East India Company crisis. Yet had he done so in the spring of 1773, such a bill likely would not have altered the selection process for local juries or limited town meetings to one a year.

The Justice Act made clear the cabinet and Parliament did not trust Massachusetts juries' honesty or temperament when it came to judging the guilt or innocence of a British official. This despite John Adams's successful defense of officer and men charged with murdering five townsmen in the "Boston Massacre," in March 1770. Adams secured acquittal of seven defendants, and a change from murder to manslaughter for the other two soldiers. By pleading "benefit of clergy" (meaning they were Christians), each of them suffered only a brand on his thumb, and then was released, with the understanding they could never again plead benefit of clergy were they convicted of another capital offense. Now, under the Justice Act, the governor could direct that a trial of an official charged with a capital offense be transferred either to another colony or to England. Curiously, at the same time, Governor Gage received formal authority to pardon any person for any crime of which he was convicted should the governor see reason to do so. The public would not have known the governor had such sweeping power, but people on both sides of the Atlantic could see the Justice Act as a serious slap in the face of Massachusetts colonists.

Colonists had a history of resenting quartering acts. Indeed, the New York government was shut down for a time when its legislature refused to appropriate funds to build barracks for British troops. Legislators argued they had not invited the troops to the colony and saw no reason to spend New Yorkers' taxes to house the troops. Eventually, imperial force showed its muscle, and the legislature capitulated.

This time, Parliament did not demand construction of barracks, but rather gave Governor Gage authority to commander taverns, unoccupied houses, and other buildings in order to house troops among the city's inhabitants. From the British perspective, this was a means of holding a threat over Bostonians' heads. No doubt, many saw this as connected to the Boston Port Bill. The troops' presence in Boston would intimidate the patriots and give them pause if they tried to maintain a haughty air as they sought to prevent payment to the East India Company for the destroyed tea.

Finally, the Quebec Act. Cabinet members were at pains to state the measure was not taken either to secure the loyalty of the French habitants if civil war broke out to the south, or to punish Americans seeking to expand into the hinterland because colonists had exerted widespread opposition to the tea tax. London journalists thought otherwise, as did opposition members in Parliament.

It matters not whether Lords Dartmouth and North had motives as pure as the driven snow in proposing the Quebec Act. Perceptions among the English and the Americans determined the act's impact on future events.

Parliament had spoken; British journalists and prominent men had judged the measures passed against Massachusetts Bay and, to a lesser extent, other colonies. How Americans responded, and if they responded with hostility, whether Britain's opinion leaders would stand with the government remained to be seen.

VII

More Thinking and Talking, Then Action

As Americans read the details of what they labeled the Intolerable Acts, they were particularly concerned that the Massachusetts Government Act overturned that colony's charter. Colony after colony stood beside the Bostonians. Then the Quebec Act's policies became public. Lurid descriptions of how Parliament intended to both force imperial tyranny and impose Catholic doctrine on American colonists living in the Ohio Valley added weight to perceived parliamentary threats against all American colonists.[171]

How would the colonists not merely blunt parliamentary assaults, but move from being on the defensive to projecting an effective offense?

Before actually addressing the need for concerted action, one rising colonial star thought a new statement of American rights and British (read Monarchical) arrogance was needed.

With the Boston Tea Party and Parliament's determination to punish the wrongdoers on his mind, young Thomas Jefferson picked up his pen and offered a new perspective on colonial rights. Elected to Virginia's House of Burgess in 1769, he soon was noticed as being both thoughtful and articulate.

Now, in 1774, Jefferson wrote a lengthy essay setting forth his arguments. In particular, he raised questions about America's relations with King George III.

Some of Jefferson's friends had the essay published as "A Summary View of the Rights of British America." Copies made their way into the hands of many who later attended the First Continental Congress. Though Jefferson did not participate directly in that Congress, delegates to it advanced Jefferson's arguments in discussions and debate, so his efforts bore fruit. Then the "Summary" set the stage for members of the Second Continental Congress to select Jefferson to write an even more stirring and important document in 1776.[172]

Written in the form of an imaginary petition to King George III, Jefferson did not mince words. He noted in the first paragraph that Americans had recoiled at "many unwarrantable encroachments and usurpations, attempted to be made by the legislature of one part of the empire, upon those rights which God and the laws have given equally and independently to all." Stating that the colonies had sent many petitions for redress of their grievances to the king, Jefferson complained that "to none of which was ever even an answer condescended...."[173]

Putting the monarch in his place, Jefferson said that the king "is no more than the chief officer of the people, appointed by the laws, and circumscribed with definite powers, to assist in working the great machine of government...." After providing an historical overview of English and British history, Jefferson gave homage to England's Saxon beginnings, deprecated the innovations flowing from the Norman invasion which William the Conqueror led, and reminded the king what two Stuart monarchs got for perpetrating tyrannical misdeeds.[174]

Jefferson addressed the issue of fair legislative representation and cabinet vetoes of colonial legislatures' efforts to provide newly populated western settlements with membership in their legislatures. He wondered whether "his majesty seriously wish, and publish to the world, that his subjects should give up the glorious right of representation, with all the benefits derived from that, and submit themselves the absolute slaves of his sovereign will?" Jefferson then took a dig at the corrupt House of Commons, in which the king and prime minister had purchased many members' votes by giving them government offices at handsome salaries: "Or is it rather meant to confine the legislative body to their present numbers, that they may be the cheaper bargain whenever they shall become worth a purchase."[175]

Then, Jefferson made clear his view on the relationship—or lack thereof—between Parliament and the colonial legislatures. He stated his position twice within the same paragraph. First, the colonists "shew that experience confirms the propriety of those political principles which exempt us from the jurisdiction of the British parliament." To make sure the king understood his imaginary message, he concluded the paragraph with the bald statement: "the British parliament has no right to exercise authority over us."[176]

In recalling Parliament's suspension of the New York legislature when that body refused to authorize funds for constructing barracks for British troops, Jefferson stated his position in yet another way: "One free and independent legislature hereby takes upon itself to suspend the powers of another, free and independent as itself...." To believe such a power existed, Jefferson said, "the principles of common sense... must be surrendered up before his majesty's subjects here can be persuaded to believe they hold their political existence at the will of a British parliament."[177]

After listing many grievances the Parliament had inflicted on the colonies, Jefferson returned to one of Cato's fears. He saved for last that fear of a standing army imposed upon them:

> Instead of subjecting the military to the civil powers, his majesty has expressly made the civil subordinate to the military. But can his majesty then put down all law under his foot? Can he erect a power superior to that which erected himself? He has done it indeed by force; but let him remember that force cannot give right.

Drawing his lengthy "petition" toward a conclusion, Jefferson reiterated that American rights were based on the idea of natural rights: "That these are our grievances which we have thus laid before his majesty, with that freedom of language and sentiment which becomes a free people claiming their rights, as derived from the laws of nature, and not as the gift of their chief magistrate." He concluded, boldly: "Let those flatter who fear; it is not an American art."[178]

While not intended to be used as a petition, the statement nevertheless was in the spirit of petitions sent to England: submissive of royal authority, but stating boldly colonial complaints and grievances. This approach represented the confident outlook many colonists maintained as a result of their, and their ancestors' experiences in America, enhanced and strengthened by their strong religious convictions. That confidence and assertiveness were exactly what the aristocrats in the cabinet and Parliament hated. People with such attitudes were not likely to yield to a "sovereign" Parliament.

Emphasizing historical precedents, but also including theoretical justifications, Jefferson's "Summary View" gave readers substantial perspective on Americans' initiative, perseverance against natural and imperial challenges, and justification for anger against a corrupt government and an autocratic king. Those who read the work in 1774 gained insight on their relations toward Britain, strength to take the perseverance about which they read and apply it to their new revolutionary situation, and a new rationale for stating their political separation from Parliament. They thus moved the dispute ever more forcefully into one of fundamental disagreements over constitutional issues.

Lord North made clear he would not consider political inferiors' claims that they held rights as Englishmen to control their own destiny. On February 20, 1775, North spoke in Parliament about a possible compromise with the Americans over the taxing issue. He had assumed, he said, the disagreement was solely over taxes. Lately he had learned that the dispute had been elevated to one of constitutionalism. If, in fact, the dispute "goes to the whole of our authority, we can enter into no negotiation, we can meet no compromise."[179]

Was trial by combat the only alternative left?

Before there was any talk about combat, Samuel Adams wanted to organize a new campaign of economic pressure on Parliament.

Sam Adams and his cohorts in the Boston Committee of Correspondence thought they knew how to challenge parliamentary authority without actually spilling blood. They drafted the "Solemn League and Covenant" which called for a complete ban of trade between the American colonies and Great Britain. Enforcement of the ban would be in the hands of those "two venerable orders of Men stiled Mechanicks and husbandmen the Strength of every Community." By doing this, any reluctant merchants would be under the watchful eye of men not involved in overseas commerce, and therefore not subject to showing favoritism to individual merchants.[180]

Wanting to build a groundswell of support for the league before publicizing it locally, the committee sent the league covenant out to communities in the New England hinterland for consideration. The proposed trade boycott would have little effect on families living a largely subsistence life. Mostly positive responses trickled back.

Then news leaked out around Boston that the Solemn League and Covenant was being discussed in farming communities but not in seaports. Naturally, a backlash occurred. Merchants demanded a retraction, and pressure built for an open meeting. But, by bringing many tradesmen and laborers to the meeting, Sam Adams and his supporters weathered the assaults and then proposed to seek other colonies' support.[181]

Letters went out from the Boston Committee of Correspondence to its counterparts in New York, Philadelphia, Charleston, and smaller towns. The responses were largely negative in one sense, but positive in another. Most respondents rejected the league boycott plan, but many suggested calling an intercolonial congress to consider Boston's plight. Interestingly, only four days after Boston asked for help, little Rhode Island led the way in promising to support Boston if others would join the cause. The patriots in Providence seem to have been first in proposing an intercolonial congress. Other colonies soon joined the call.[182]

Initially, Adams and other Boston patriots were lukewarm about the proposed congress, fearing it would take too long to organize to have any effective influence on Parliament or the king. In less than a month, though, they warmed to the idea, perhaps changing their attitude when they realized a general congress could be brought together in Philadelphia in September.

Colony after colony decided to participate in a continental congress. Only Georgia held back.

The process colonial leaders followed to reach that decision and then select delegates to represent their colony at the congress initiated the final breakdown of British government in America.[183]

Meanwhile, Thomas Hutchinson was on his way to London. He left Boston on June 1, the day the Port Act went into effect. General Gage succeeded him as Governor.

A veteran military officer who had some experience in politics as a Member of Parliament, Gage was strangely naive to colonists' intrigues. Wily patriots easily fooled him. This despite the fact he had spent twenty years in America as a British military commander. He had called the legislature into session in Salem based on false intelligence that legislative leaders were pursuing a moderate agenda.[184]

On June 17, Sam Adams, secretary to the assembly, had the doors of the legislature's room locked and the key removed. Then he and his fellow patriots called for a general continental congress to meet in Philadelphia on September 1. The legislature approved this resolution, named Sam, his cousin John, and three other prominent men to represent Massachusetts Bay at the congress. The legislature then devised a plan to fund its delegates' expenses.[185]

When Governor Gage learned what the legislature was up to, he signed a pronouncement dissolving it. He was too late. By the time the legislators unlocked the doors, the deeds were done. So, too, was the Massachusetts Bay legislature. It never met again.

In Virginia, the House of Burgesses was meeting when the Virginia Gazette published a summary of the Boston Port Act on May 19. That edition also printed a rumor that Sam Adams, John Hancock, and several others were to be arrested and shipped to London for trial. Some members of the Burgesses called for a discussion on how Virginia would aid Boston. They were overruled with the argument the legislature had to complete its pressing domestic agenda before considering Boston's fate.[186]

As the date for closing Boston's port neared, several members of the Burgesses persuaded a prominent conservative leader to introduce a resolution calling on Virginians to hold June 1 as a day of fasting and prayer in support of the people of Boston. Shortly after this, Governor Dunmore dissolved the legislature for impinging on his power. Only the governor, he said, could issue such a proclamation.

The day after Governor Dunmore canceled the legislative session, eighty-nine members of the Burgesses met in Raleigh Tavern to consider Virginia's response to the Port Act. Those present chose Peyton Randolph, who had been Speaker of the House of Burgesses, as their moderator. They quickly adopted resolutions condemning British policies. Then they proposed an Association and agreed to boycott all East India Company products, though they did not call for a general boycott of British goods. The group next asked the committee of correspondence of the old legislature to write its counterparts in other colonies and propose a general congress.[187]

Following the rump session's adjournment, a letter from Sam Adams arrived in Williamsburg asking for Virginia's support. Peyton Randolph notified those Burgesses still in town to attend another meeting the following day. By that time only twenty-five were present. Concluding the small group could not speak for the colony, they issued a call for all the former members to attend a conference in Williamsburg some two months later, on August 1.

Many county leaders considered the issues and the threats too pressing merely to stand by, wait two months, and watch. Over the months of June and July, county after county after county held mass meetings at which citizens passed resolutions and chose delegates to the August colony-wide meeting.

When that gathering convened on August 1, representatives from all but one of Virginia's sixty-one counties were present. They quickly agreed to a nonimportation policy, along with a colony-wide boycott of British goods, known as the association. Local representatives were expected to enforce the boycott. Delegates also called for a congress and elected a seven-member delegation to that congress.[188]

The association's formation was a major step in Virginia's move to a revolutionary government. Though the association spoke as a colony, it was to act at the local level. Local leaders had taken charge of organizing protest groups to write resolutions and pick delegates to the August 1 convention. Now they took charge of organizing local inspectors to see that merchants and storekeepers honored the boycott of British goods. Should local inspectors find violators of the association, they were to publicize that information and thus penalize those in violation. In doing so, they would be overriding the authority of duly constituted county sheriffs, constables, and justices of the peace. Ironically, some of those acting under aegis of the association also held county judicial offices. In a very real sense, revolutionary change in government was beginning at the local level.[189]

During that August where stirring rhetoric elevated typical Virginia summer heat, George Washington, considered a "moderate" by many, gave evidence his determination was as strong as other patriots. He wrote:

> I could wish, I own, that the dispute had been left to posterity to determine, but the crisis is arrived when we must assert our rights, or submit to every imposition, that can be heaped upon us, till custom and use shall make us as

tame and abject slaves, as the blacks we rule over with such arbitrary sway. [190]

As Virginians developed their plans and systems, other colonies were working to accomplish similar goals. Maryland, South Carolina, and North Carolina navigated their separate ways through issues and politics. Indeed, as early as the first week of June, Christopher Gadsden, a prominent South Carolina patriot, wrote to the Boston Committee of Correspondence: "A Congress seems to be much wish'd for here. The Determination of that wou'd have the greatest Weight." He strengthened his argument by informing the Boston Committee that Charleston was shipping almost 200 barrels of rice to Boston for distribution to those who "may be thought to stand in need of immediate Assistance...."

From South Carolina north, all colonies eventually established principles and chose delegates to an intercolonial congress. Again, voluntary meetings at the local level provided candidates for colony-wide conventions. In North Carolina, the convention met in the face of the governor's pronouncement that such a gathering was illegal.[191]

Further north, local politics took precedence over concerns about "rights." In Pennsylvania, patriot leaders eager to support Boston as it faced its plight found themselves opposed by a powerful Quaker political faction. Conservative Quaker merchants indicated they were willing to watch Boston radicals stew in their own briny tea.[192]

Philadelphia's patriot leaders were eager to push for support of Boston, criticism of Parliament, and a call for a congress. To succeed they decided they should have a prominent conservative Pennsylvanian lead the charge. John Dickinson seemed just the man. A very prosperous lawyer, Dickinson had made a name for himself in Pennsylvania and, indeed, throughout the colonies during 1767-68 with his "Letters from a Pennsylvania Farmer," in which he attacked the Townshend Duties. He also had gained a seat in the legislature, overcoming the vigorous opposition of the Speaker of the House and leader of the Quaker party, Joseph Galloway. After giving strict instructions as to an agenda and speakers, Dickinson agreed to attend and speak at a mass meeting.[193]

A small but economically and politically powerful crowd met in mid-May to consider Boston's plight. Dickinson did his part, offering a strong concluding speech in which he endorsed a previously proposed call to the governor to convene the legislature so it could petition Parliament. Then the crowd of around three hundred citizens chose a Committee of Correspondence to answer Boston's call for help. The committee met and drafted a letter criticizing the Tea Party's destruction of private property, calling for Boston to reimburse the East India Company for its loss, but also agreeing to support a continental congress. Philadelphia's patriot leaders no doubt had hoped for a better result from their efforts, but they were still in the game.

When neither the Committee of Correspondence nor Governor Penn took action to hold a colony-wide convention or call the legislature into session, the patriots planned a mass meeting of mechanics. This prompted the Committee to call a citywide meeting. The Committee then got a step up on the patriots by developing an agenda in detail for the meeting. At that meeting Dickinson agreed to head a new Committee of Correspondence charged with appealing to county leaders to select delegates to a Pennsylvania-wide meeting. At that point, Governor Penn called the legislature into session.

Delegates from across the colony met to pass resolutions and write instructions for those chosen to represent Pennsylvania at the continental congress, which was to meet in their capital of Philadelphia. Even though the Quaker party dominated the legislature, delegates to the convention agreed that the legislature should choose representatives to the continental congress. The legislature did so, voting for a thoroughly conservative slate led by Speaker of the House Joseph Galloway. Galloway also saw that instructions he wrote for the delegates to follow replaced the convention's instructions. Seemingly, the conservatives had trumped the patriots—except those conservative delegates now had to attend the continental congress as Pennsylvania's representatives, and had to abide by the declarations and policies the congress approved.[194]

New York's warring De Lancey and Livingston parties competed with each other to dominate the colony's response to Boston's appeal for help. As the party currently out of power in the legislature, the Livingstons backed the city's Sons of Liberty when it called a meeting to discuss Boston's appeal. Perhaps showing why they were still in power, De Lancey's forces dominated the meeting and organized a fifty-one-member Committee of Correspondence. While giving the Livingstons and the patriots some seats on the committee, the conservative De Lancey forces controlled it. After writing a general letter of support to Boston, it called for a general colonial congress.

The next step was selecting delegates to the congress. This provoked intense partisan conflict. When the De Lancey majority on the committee of Fifty-one overwhelmed the Livingston minority and selected five conservatives to represent New York in the Philadelphia congress, Livingston partisans began a newspaper war, accompanied by pressure from a mechanics group, for an alternative slate of delegates. Negotiations between the warring factions generated a compromise, and the De Lancey slate of delegates won a popular election on July 28.

The long-and-short of the political battles in New York was similar to that in Pennsylvania. The conservative De Lancey faction controlled the colony's delegation to the continental congress, but the patriots, with help from the Livingston faction, forced the conservatives to, first, agree to the congress, and, second, support a boycott of British goods if the congress called for a boycott.[195]

Delaware patriots had no difficulty organizing a delegation to the congress, because it was overwhelmingly an agricultural colony and because its governor was the Pennsylvania governor and therefore an absentee. In New Jersey, Governor Franklin (estranged son of Benjamin Franklin) strongly opposed the patriots. He refused to call the Assembly into session, apparently thinking this would keep the colony out of the congress. The patriots brought about county committee meetings, which chose delegates to a colony-wide convention scheduled for July. At that three-day conference, the seventy-two attendees wrote a series of resolutions denying Parliament's right to tax the colonies, and declaring: "The claim of the British Parliament…to make laws, which shall be binding on the king's American subjects 'in all cases whatsoever', and particularly for imposing taxes, for the purpose of raising a revenue in America, is unconstitutional and oppressive." Attendees also endorsed a general congress, and chose five delegates to represent New Jersey at the congress. So much for Governor Franklin's effort to control politics in the colony.[196]

New Hampshire's patriots gained wide, popular support for a colony-wide meeting, and those who attended ignored the governor's personal attempt to intervene. They, too, chose delegates to the congress. Connecticut and Rhode Island, twin bastions of republicanism as corporate colonies, had popularly elected governors. For them, then, support for Boston and for a general congress came as a matter of course.[197]

Only Georgia, of "the original thirteen" failed to commit itself to sending representatives to the general congress. Less than forty years old, and originally founded as a "prisoner" colony, Georgia had relatively few inhabitants. It faced Indian warfare on its western front, which involved some British redcoats, and was so poor it relied on British subsidies to keep its government operating.

Popular opinion generally saw Governor Wright as being a responsible official. All these factors put Georgia's patriot leaders at a distinct disadvantage. They were able to generate a general meeting to consider Boston's plight. At that meeting they secured resolutions condemning the coercive acts and pledging the Colony's endorsement of all "constitutional" measures to redress colonial grievances with Parliament. But the delegates did not vote to send representatives to a general congress.[198]

By mid-August, twelve colonies had chosen delegates to a continental congress. The contest between Parliament and the colonies was at least balanced at this point, though Bostonians and their supporters in the northeast were doing what they could to harry Governor Gage and tip the balance in the colonists' favor.

Informed via letter by Secretary for the American Department, Lord Dartmouth, that he should rule Boston and Massachusetts "by temper and prudence on the one hand and by firmness and resolution on the other," when he received this advice on August 6, 1774, Governor/General Gage must have scratched his head in wonder at the Secretary's disconnect with reality. Only beginning his third month in office after taking over the governorship from Thomas Hutchinson, Gage was wondering if he could govern at all.

Under the recently passed Massachusetts Government Act, Parliament decreed that members of the governor's council no longer would be elected, but rather receive their appointments from the Crown. A list of thirty-six names for a new governor's council came to Gage. When informed of their appointments, twelve immediately resigned. Once the list of those accepting became public, several additional councilors resigned, including former Governor Hutchinson's son. Some newly appointed councilors fled to Castle William for protection. Governor Gage, who by now had been harassed out of Salem and had returned to Boston, reported to London that he could not call the legislature into session in Salem without ordering out British troops to protect those still willing to serve in the upper house.[199]

Other elements of the Massachusetts Bay government also were disintegrating. Mobs in the western counties prevented county courts from sitting. When the Superior Court ordered men to appear either as grand jurors or trial jurors, the men appeared, but refused to take the required oath, thus preventing the Court from proceeding. Popular leaders in the hinterland called out militia units, ordered the government-appointed company and field officers to resign, then told the militiamen to elect new officers.

Towns received directions to stockpile armaments and secure field pieces. Militia companies chose minutemen with orders to have their weapons ready for immediate action.[200]

When General Gage ordered defensive breastworks built around the narrow neck that connected the Boston peninsula to the mainland, those men hired for the job quickly learned their neighbors did not want them to continue working for the British. They abandoned their jobs. Similarly, when Gage hired workmen to build barracks for the troops, those who started the project soon found a need to withdraw their services. Patriots in nearby towns, and, indeed, as far south as New York, saw that neither labor nor materials were made available to the British in Boston. Eventually, General Gage managed to recruit fifty workers from Nova Scotia to complete the fortifications and the barracks. The soldiers did not get into their new quarters until November. By that time, Gage was Governor in name only. Local patriot committee actions swallowed up all semblance of Crown authority in Massachusetts. More ominous, a provincial convention was about to meet. Plenty of dry tinder was available to start a fire if someone or some group struck a spark.[201]

VIII

Feeling Their Way toward Unity While Still Professing Loyalty

In late August 1774, men traveled north to Philadelphia from South Carolina, Virginia, and Maryland; and south from New England, New York, and New Jersey. They were on their way to participate in America's first general congress. Though nine colonies had sent delegates to the Stamp Act Congress, which met in New York in October 1765, the agenda was limited to issues relating to the Stamp Act. Delegates from twelve colonies were to be at this new congress. They had a general agenda: determining American rights, how Parliament was trampling on those rights, and how the colonies should respond.

As delegates traveled to Philadelphia, leaders from towns through which they passed hosted them. Those town leaders flattered the delegates by the attention and accommodations they showered on them. Yet beyond flattery, the delegates benefited by picking up intelligence about those with whom they were soon to engage in discussion, debate, and compromise.

While colonial delegates were making their way to Philadelphia, on August 24 King George III was proposing to his prime minister, Lord North, that Parliament be dissolved, and elections called for a new House of Commons. Though elections were not mandated until March 1775, the king had the prerogative of dissolving a Parliament and calling elections at any time. In this case, he proposed to have the North administration make secret plans for the election before announcing the date in order to place opposition factions at a disadvantage. One reason he gave for wanting fall elections was that news regarding decisions of the "general Congress now assembled in America" would not reach England for some months, and the administration would be at an advantage if the Congress's statements and actions were not known at election time. This would allow the "king's friends"—men who held seats in the Commons because the king or his well-placed aristocratic allies controlled the votes in a Commons district—to give aid to other administration supporters who might need assistance to win reelection.[202]

A number of prominent Americans living in London had forecast earlier in the year that the electorate might show massive rejection of the North administration in the next parliamentary election, leading to someone replacing him as prime minister who was prepared to meet the colonists' demands for imperial reform.

The king's strategy was to hold the election at a time when the electorate would not be focusing on the colonies. Then those relatively few Commons races that were in doubt could be contested largely on domestic issues.

Although reluctant to risk his comfortable majority, Lord North realized that holding off the elections until the following spring could be a mistake, so he signaled his willingness to have Parliament dissolved immediately. He made a wise choice.

King George dissolved Parliament on September 30, 1774, and ordered a new legislature to convene on November 29, 1774. This left a campaign of exactly sixty days.[203]

Not a vigorous campaigner himself, Lord North was able to use the month of September to prepare for the election before the king dissolved Parliament. Among his more concrete plans was the infusion of cash in certain districts to help favored candidates. He had the Treasury spend around 50,000 pounds sterling on selected races. North also placed favored men in seats the government "controlled." Because members were not required to live in the district they "represented," he told one of his supporters: "you may suddenly hear you are duly elected for a Borough you do not think of." Further, the short notice of the election caught the opposition factions unprepared, which George III had forecast.

The parliamentary elections resulted, as North wrote to the king, in a substantial victory. Lord North calculated that when Parliament reconvened, he would have 321 firm supporters in the Commons, as for a mix of opposition and fence sitters of 237. The administration's backers in the Commons included 170 members who had received financially lucrative posts within the government.[204]

In the House of Lords, whose members held their positions through titles rather than election, the king or the government had seen that seventy of the peers were on the government payroll.[205]

Americans living in London had badly miscalculated the British people's mood when they forecast that North would suffer severe losses in the election. Richard Henry Lee wrote in the spring of 1774 that "The wise and good in Britain are too well convinced of the unmerited abuse we have received for ten or twelve years past not to produce consequences from a dispute with America, fatal to the views of Ministry at a General Election." He and several other Americans in London had made the mistake of generalizing from conversations they had with men who, perhaps for economic reasons, expressed sympathy for the colonies. Indeed, after the election there were indications that those who had used "the American question" in their campaigns had fared less well than those who entirely ignored the colonies. British intellectual and member of Parliament Edmund Burke had observed in February 1774, when news of the Boston Tea Party was still percolating through the newspapers, that Britons were uninterested in colonial issues: "Any remarkable highway robbery on Hounslow Heath would make more conversation than all the disturbances of America."[206]

However one reads the election results, King George III and his lieutenant, Lord North, looked forward to being able to push through Parliament whatever policies they wished. That included rigorously maintaining the argument of parliamentary supremacy over the colonies. Now they had to wait for news from Philadelphia before planning their next moves.

The month-long lag time in sending information across the Atlantic worked to the North administration's advantage in keeping the fall elections focused on domestic issues. For those about to attend the Continental Congress, the reverse was not a factor. They were decidedly inward looking, focusing on Americans' liberties and current threats to them.

Except for the few who had developed a coterie of intercolonial correspondents over the previous decade, most delegates were virtually unknown to those outside their own colony.

Those who maintained written communication with fellow patriots in other colonies had never met their literary friends in person. This was where the slow pace of travel allowed men heading for Philadelphia to ferret out the sentiments of others with whom they soon would be exchanging ideas and, on occasion, thrusting and parrying with intellectual swords.

Massachusetts delegates learned about the diversity of opinions regarding themselves and those representing other New England colonies, as well as the middle colonies. For example, when the Massachusetts entourage entered New Haven, Connecticut, a large parade of carriages and horsemen ushered them into town. The Massachusetts delegation was much impressed by the hospitality and warm reception. Only later did they learn that "the Parade which was made, to introduce Us into Town was a Sudden Proposal, in order to divert the Populace from erecting a Liberty Pole &c."[207] Erecting a liberty pole would have implied support for radical, even possibly "democratical" ideas. Those organizing the parade favored moderate reactions to recent British aggression against Boston and Massachusetts. This told the Massachusetts men something of the sentiment they might find in members of the Connecticut delegation when they met them in Philadelphia.

The Massachusetts delegation received further cautions during a stay of several days in New York City.

Alexander McDougall, one of a triumvirate of middle-class radical patriot leaders in New York City, spent many hours with John Adams. He had been kept off the New York delegation to the Congress, largely because of his radical views. McDougall

> gave a Caution to avoid every Expression here, which looked like an Allusion to the last Appeal. He says there is a powerful Party here, who are intimidated by Fears of a Civil War, and they have been induced to acquiesce by Assurance that there was no Danger, and that a peaceful Cessation of Commerce would effect Relief.

In addition, McDougall warned that some influential New Yorkers "are intimidated lest the leveling Spirit of the New England Colonies should propagate itself into N[ew] York."

Upon the Massachusetts delegation's arrival in Philadelphia, a prominent local patriot took Sam Adams and his colleagues into a quiet room. He warned them that some Boston loyalists had sent warnings to Philadelphia that Samuel Adams could not be trusted. The Philadelphian warned the Massachusetts men: "You must not utter the word independence, nor give the least hint or insinuation of the idea either in congress or in any private conversation.... No man dares speak of it." The New Englanders took these warnings to heart, and remained reticent during the early days of the Congress, to good effect.[208]

Cautious men with moderate to conservative political views dominated both the New York and Pennsylvania delegations. They used the weekend before Congress opened on September 5 to lobby other delegates. In this they were not alone. Sam Adams remained reserved in public, but practiced his organizing skills among Virginia and South Carolina delegations' radical patriot leaders. They, in turn, felt out others who had similar sentiments.

Then they agreed on "housekeeping" details, which they advanced the next day.[209]

Delegates met in a local Philadelphia tavern, with the intention of selecting a permanent meeting place. Joseph Galloway, conservative Quaker and powerful speaker of Pennsylvania's lower house, grandly offered the Pennsylvania State House. Local tradesmen countered Galloway's invitation by inviting the delegates to use Carpenter's Hall. As Sam Adams and his new friends hoped, the delegates agreed to look over Carpenter's Hall first. Then, having seen it, some argued it would suit the Congress's needs. Without inspecting the State House, and over strenuous objections from some Pennsylvania and New York delegates, the majority voted to settle down in Carpenter's Hall.

Score one for the Massachusetts patriot Sam Adams.[210]

Peyton Randolph's reputation as a thoughtful, temperate speaker of Virginia's House of Burgesses made him an easy choice for "president" of the Congress. An influential delegate from Connecticut thought Randolph "seems designed by nature for the business." That left the post of secretary. Thomas Lynch of South Carolina nominated Charles Thomson of Philadelphia. Though not a member of the Congress, he was duly elected, again to the chagrin of Joseph Galloway, who branded Thomson as "one of the most violent Sons of Liberty... in America." (Thomson, in fact, served as secretary throughout both continental congresses and the Confederation Congress.)[211]

A proposal to begin daily meetings with a prayer brought objections that delegates represented too many denominations for that to be a useful exercise. Sam Adams, known for some fiery denunciations of the Church of England (Anglicanism), suggested that a blessing from any of God's messengers would be welcome, and nominated a prominent Philadelphia Anglican minister. Shocking some of his critics into compliance, delegates accepted his suggestion. The next morning the Reverend Mister Douche presented what Sam's cousin John considered: "A Prayer, which he gave us of his own Composition, was as pertinent, as affectionate, as sublime, as devout, as I ever heard offered up to Heaven." Delegates would need such inspiration on a regular basis if they were to succeed in the tasks they set for themselves, and, indeed, John Adams later attended one of Rev. Douche's worship services, declaring him to be "a fine preacher, indeed."[212]

Forty of the fifty-six delegates to the First Continental Congress had experience as colonial legislators, and at least ten of them had served as speaker of their lower house. They understood the deliberative process, and proceeded to apply their knowledge and skills to addressing the issues facing them, but they did so with no desire to rush through to decisions on those issues. Indeed, to the chagrin of a few who favored action over words, some delegates gave lengthy speeches on topics that others had laid out clearly and succinctly. As John Adams observed:

> There is no greater Mortification than to sit with half a dozen Witts, deliberating upon a Petition, Address, or Memorial. These great Witts, these subtle Criticks, these refined Genius's, these learned Lawyers, these wise Statesmen, are so fond of shewing their Parts and Powers, as to make their Consultations very tedious.[213]

Flowery rhetoric may have slowed the process of determining intercolonial policies and adopting petitions for the redress of grievances, but it provided opportunities for energetic politicians among the delegates to negotiate and plot strategies for winning acceptance of their doctrines. The radical patriots proved adept at gaining the upper hand, though they had to engage in considerable give-and-take with delegates whose perspectives were less assertive than theirs.

An early decision, one accompanied with considerable contention, was how votes were to be taken. Few questioned the wisdom of having votes by colony rather than individual, but should "large" colonies, such as Virginia and Pennsylvania, which were quite populous, have more votes than "small" colonies such as Maryland or Delaware? Though grudgingly given, diplomacy won out. Delegates agreed each colony was to have one vote, determined by a majority of its delegates. Even this arrangement eventually created some embarrassing problems when, on critically important issues, delegates in a colony split evenly on how to vote, thus resulting in an abstention.[214]

Giving a nod to moderates' sensibilities, the Congress decided first to prepare a statement of colonial rights and how the British government had violated those rights. The Congress might have resolved itself into a committee of the whole, but chose instead to appoint a committee to prepare the document. Each colony (of which at this point eleven had representatives in Philadelphia) selected two members to serve on it. But a committee of twenty-two was not much more efficient or less contentious than would have been one of the whole. Then, when the twelfth colony's representatives arrived—those of North Carolina on September 14—the committee expanded to twenty-four. Meanwhile, as committee members argued, debated, lobbied each other, the remaining delegates fussed and fumed in frustration, waiting to read the committee's masterpiece. They waited some time.[215]

Beginning its work on September 8, 1774, committee members labored for two days over the basis of colonial rights. Radical patriots favored basing their rights on natural law, the British constitution, the separate colonial charters, and "immemorial Usage." Moderates and legalists opposed claiming natural rights, arguing they were too vague to pin down.[216]

Perhaps realizing the large committee would struggle indefinitely to formulate a written doctrine, it first agreed to base colonial rights on natural rights, the British Constitution, and on charters and compacts. Then it appointed a small subcommittee to write the statement. Doing so took the delegates some time, though they worked six days a week. After reporting back to the committee, members agreed to a final draft and submitted it to the Congress on September 22. A second statement addressing British infringement of those rights was handed to Congress two days later.[217]

In the mean time, those not involved in the small writing group didn't just fiddle around.

The Boston contingent had left instructions with Dr. Joseph Warren, one of the foremost patriots in Bean Town, to organize a county meeting and formulate a statement regarding American rights. By having a Suffolk County meeting rather than a Boston Town Meeting, participants would not be violating the Massachusetts Government Act which limited town meetings to one a year, but which failed to restrict county meetings.

Dr. Warren, in consultation with Sam Adams before the latter left for Philadelphia, had prepared a stirring defense of American rights and a resounding rejection of parliamentary authority over the colonies. While the statement acknowledged the supremacy of the king, it stated such supremacy was by "compact." Denouncing Parliament's recent oppressive legislation, he advocated a trade boycott to force its revocation. He added a statement that colonists should be prepared to fight for their land, but only in a defensive cause.[218]

Suffolk County residents met in Milton on September 9, 1774, and approved the resolutions. All that was fine for the people of Boston and Suffolk County, but many other resolutions had been passed in towns and counties up and down the colonies throughout the summer and fall. How could these resolves generate greater interest?

Paul Revere answered that question. He left Boston shortly after the resolves had been adopted and spent a week of hard riding to hand a copy to the Massachusetts delegation on September 16. The next day, the delegation presented the Suffolk Resolves to the Congress.

Fortunately for the Adams cousins another, independently posted message, arrived from Boston before the Resolves were read. It claimed that British troops had gone to Charlestown, located across the Charles River from Boston, to confiscate military supplies the patriots had been stockpiling there. In the process, the message said, the soldiers had killed six civilians. This caused great fear and worry among the delegates. A corrective message followed, confirming that British troops had confiscated military supplies, but reported that no gunfire had ensued, and no one had been killed, wounded, or arrested. Yet the news of aggressive British military action against the colonists moved additional delegates toward the radical side.

The Suffolk Resolves shocked many moderates at the congress. Some considered them the equivalent of a declaration of independence, but when debate began over whether the Congress should adopt the resolves, those in opposition found themselves in a very tight place.

No one kept notes of the debates over adopting the Suffolk Resolves, but a few written reactions and later memoirs suggest the kinds of questions the patriots must have asked: Had colonies submitted numerous petitions for redress of their grievances only to have those petitions haughtily rejected or ignored? Had Parliament passed Intolerable Acts which oppressed Boston and Massachusetts, and set precedents for oppressing people in all the colonies? Had Parliament, through the Quebec Act, installed an autocratic government over the entire Ohio Valley region, denying future access to settlers from Virginia, Pennsylvania, and New York? Had the king's government taken control of the Massachusetts courts, making judges obligated to that government for their salaries and their continuance in office, and therefore obligated to favor that government when disputes arose concerning the king's policies? Should colonists meekly submit to Royal tyranny or military might? To vote for the Suffolk Resolves was to stand up against Royal and parliamentary acts of tyranny. To vote against those Resolves was to favor submission to Parliament and to the king's ministers as those ministers ran roughshod over American rights.

So, an intense debate preceded a decision on whether the Congress should endorse the Resolves. Then each colony's delegates caucused to determine how that colony would vote. Many delegates apparently wanted Congress to reject the Resolves, but not so many as to cause any colony to cast a negative vote. When the verbal smoke cleared, the Continental Congress had voted "unanimously" to endorse the Suffolk Resolves, and ordered them printed and distributed.

Despite sharp internal divisions, the Congress presented a facade of unanimity. Score another victory for those who had demanded the colonies cast one vote each on all questions brought before the Congress.[219]

Congress's adoption of the Suffolk County Resolves was more an act of propaganda than a firm declaration of principles. Yet having adopted them, members found themselves tilting more heavily toward the ideas behind those Resolves. Even as discussion continued over a declaration of rights, others pressed for action. On September 22, Congress had printed an announcement to all merchants to not place any further orders for goods from Great Britain. It also suggested that, where possible, previous orders be canceled. After almost five days of haggling over when and how nonimportation of goods should be effected, delegates decided that December 1 would be the date to halt British imports. Added to this was a recommendation to citizens that they not purchase goods merchants brought into their stores from Britain after December 1.[220]

Moderate delegates hoped a counterattack might carry the day. Joseph Galloway rose to speak on September 28. He laid out a plan for placing the colonies in a quasi-independent condition within the empire. Colonies would select delegates to a grand council that would have power to legislate for the colonies in general, but not for individual colonies. Each colony would maintain independent authority with respect to its internal affairs. The king would name a president general to preside over the council, who would serve at the king's pleasure. Parliament would remain the supreme legislature of the empire, but no measure Parliament passed affecting the colonies would be made law until the grand council endorsed it.[221]

This plan made rational sense if one were willing to forgive and forget the increasingly rigid parliamentary and ministerial policies that were fixated on requiring colonies to submit to British dictates and acknowledge parliamentary supremacy "in all cases whatsoever." Few, if any, of the ardent patriots were of such a forgiving—or trusting—mind.

Americans knew through the press that some strong voices in Parliament had been counseling patience, toleration, and moderation in Britain's dealings with the American colonies. Might the Galloway plan allow the old and new worlds to return to a happy relationship? Patriots thought not, perhaps because they knew those strong parliamentary voices counseling a moderate, accommodating approach to the colonial crisis were consistently outvoted by more than two-to-one in both the Commons and the Lords. Yet the Galloway plan offered the best alternative between colonial submission to parliamentary dominance and complete colonial separation from the Empire. Surely, plan supporters argued, it was worth proposing to Britain. By doing so, members of the Congress could determine the North administration's sincerity in seeking an accommodating solution to the crisis. Such an argument placed the patriots in a box. To support the proposal would derail the initiative patriots held and delay further action until a response could be secured from London—a delay of at least three months. Yet those who opposed the plan could be charged with working for independence, something none of them was willing to acknowledge publicly. Patriot politicians offered a third alternative.

Voting by colonies, delegates decided six-to-five, with one abstention, to table the Galloway plan of union for later discussion. That later discussion never was held, and when the minutes of Congress were published, no reference to the Galloway plan appeared in them.[222]

With moderates both defeated and dispirited, patriots moved forward on a number of pending items: approving a declaration of rights; determining when to begin nonimportation of British goods; when nonexport of American goods to Britain and the British West Indies should start; fashioning a petition to the king; and writing appeals to the people of England, to Quebec, and to their fellow Americans. Not surprisingly, deciding on whether and then when to have nonimport and nonexport of goods take effect generated sharp differences between merchants and planters. Accompanying these contests were disagreements as to what should be banned from import and export. Debate degenerated into name-calling, and delegate suspicion of others' motives came into the fore. Yet they struggled on.[223]

Practical disagreements over what to include in product bans, whether temperate or emotional, were based on personal experience and individual concern with related financial issues. Eventually, delegates resolved their disagreements and made decisions to stop importing goods from Britain on December 1, 1774, and stop exporting goods to Britain and the British West Indies on September 10, 1775. The later date for stopping exports was a nod to southern planters, who already had harvested their 1774 tobacco crop, but would not have it dried and cured for export for another eight months or so.[224]

A serious hurdle members still had to overcome involved political theory. It related to one provision in the declaration of rights. Did Parliament have a "right" to regulate the empire's trade, or were colonies granting Parliament permission to regulate trade for their mutual benefit? Extended debate and repeated, unsuccessful efforts to fashion an acceptable statement demonstrated the seriousness and the depth of thought delegates had given to their position's ideological base. Following two days of debate, the Congress considered whether to acknowledge or withhold parliamentary power over the regulation of trade. A tie vote resulted. John Adams then took on the task of writing a statement that would break the impasse. He fashioned one in which voluntary acknowledgment held sway.

Since colonists could not be represented in Parliament, colonial legislatures had complete power over internal legislation and taxation, subject only to the king's veto. Of a practical matter, a uniform regulation of trade was desirable. Therefore, as long as the measures were narrowly limited to the regulation of that trade, and provided no tax or duty was levied for raising revenue, the colonies: "cheerfully consent to the operation of such acts of the British Parliament...." With this thorny issue settled, Congress adopted its declaration of rights and grievances on October 14.[225]

A final action involved authorizing the association to enforce boycott restrictions. In the debate over this, several South Carolina delegates declared their unwillingness to support the association because it called for banning the export of indigo and rice to any port. If northern colonies could ship wheat, flour, fish, and other products to southern Europe or non-British West Indies, why couldn't South Carolinians ship rice there? Indigo, admittedly, was a different matter, since Britain was its principal market. They had a point, and delegates from the northern colonies acknowledged it. Rice was removed from the banned list. Work on fashioning the association continued.[226]

Colonies were to see that every county, city, and town formed compliance committees to enforce the boycotts. In addition, the Congress admonished citizens to promote local agricultural and manufacturing production, always keeping profits modest and making accommodations for those in financial distress. They also were encouraged to forsake riotous public living, avoiding such diversions as horse racing, plays, and similar public spectacles. Frugality and simplicity were to be the standards sought.[227]

All that remained for Congress was to tidy up some declarations, see they were published and distributed, and decide on future action. This last came on October 22, when delegates voted to call on the provincial legislatures or assemblies to select delegates to a second Congress, which was to convene on May 10, 1775. On October 26, 1774, fifty-one days after it convened, the First Continental Congress resolved itself into history.[228]

How would London react to its pronouncements? In fact, that question already was being answered. Lord North had correspondents in Philadelphia who were sending him the bits and pieces coming out of the Congress as they became available.[229]

Lord Dartmouth had looked upon the Congress—illegal though he thought it was—as a possible link in creating an acceptable settlement of the disputes between mother country and recalcitrant colonies. "I am not without hope," he wrote on August 31, 1774, "that some good may arise out of it... if it should chalk out any reasonable line of accommodation, or make any moderate or temperate proposal...." His problem was that a majority of the Congressional delegates had little interest in "temperate" proposals. This he learned when he saw a copy of the Suffolk Resolves, along with a published announcement that Congress had been "unanimous" in endorsing those Resolves.

Former Massachusetts Governor Hutchinson visited Lord Dartmouth shortly after Dartmouth had read the Resolves, and wrote that Dartmouth was "thunderstruck" with what he had read. To him the Resolves seemed equivalent to a declaration of war, a view the moderate Continental Congress delegate Joseph Galloway of Pennsylvania shared. Even so, this did not stop Dartmouth from following developments in the Congress by way of a secret correspondent who reported to him from Philadelphia.[230]

By the time members of the North administration received copies of Congress's declarations; letters to British, American, and Quebec inhabitants; and the petition to the king, they also were faced with reports from General Gage that Massachusetts was bordering on rebellion. There seemed no avenue open to compromise. Still, Dartmouth was determined to try.

In mid-December, Lord North proposed to the king that the government suspend payment of all bounties and regulations designed to benefit trade from the colonies, while also implementing a plan Dartmouth proposed. That was to send a commission to America to negotiate with colonial leaders. The king endorsed cancellation of trade policies favorable to the colonies, but soundly rejected the idea of a commission. He argued that such a step would indicate "the mother country being more afraid of the continuance of the dispute than the colonies and I cannot think it likely to make them reasonable...I do not want to drive them to despair but to submission...."[231]

The only apparent hope remaining for a peaceful resolution of the conflict was with the king. He had not yet reacted to the petition Congress had submitted to him, and would not likely do so until Parliament returned from its leisurely Christmas vacation.

Congress's declaration of rights, its letter to the British people, and the association had made their way into Britain's press. Their publication motivated a new rash of petitions within Britain.

Merchants and manufacturers in England's industrial cities began sending petitions to Parliament pleading for relief for the Americans, and expressing fear for their business solvency if the Americans implemented effective boycotts. Some of these were spontaneous acts which local business leaders initiated; members of the parliamentary opposition stimulated others. Whatever the petitions' sources, spokesmen for the North administration denigrated them as coming either from dupes of the colonists or from those who were actually disloyal to the government.

Recognizing that a political war was under way, cabinet members and other government supporters persuaded several key business leaders to petition Parliament on behalf of the government's position. They demanded that colonial economic pressure be resisted.[232]

When Parliament reconvened, the government saw that petitions favorable to its position on the colonies were sent to a previously appointed committee to study American documents. Those supporting concessions to the colonies went to a committee Edmund Burke called a "Coventry committee," meaning parliamentary leaders would see the petitions were ignored. This still left unknown the king's reaction to the Continental Congress's petition.[233]

Despite its being sent to him, the king simply forwarded the petition, without comment, to Parliament. Lord North arranged for a mass of papers dealing with the colonial conflicts to be submitted to Parliament. The petition to the king was the bottom paper in the pile. When questioned, Lord North admitted he had not read the papers.[234]

Benjamin Franklin, Arthur Lee, and William Bollan, who had transmitted the Congressional petition to Lord Dartmouth in order to have the king read it, now requested the House of Commons allow them a hearing on the petition. The Commons rejected their request by a vote of 218 to 68. Neither the king nor Parliament would consider the Americans' position. From this point on, little hope remained for a negotiated settlement of the two sides' differences, though both were to try again.[235]

The king's and Prime Minister North's intransigence is an indication that had the Continental Congress approved Joseph Galloway's plan to create a colonial parliament, and sent that proposal to London, it would have been rejected almost out of hand.

General Gage determined the future course of conflict between Britain and the colonies. On April 19, 1775, he sent a large detachment of troops out of Boston to confiscate military supplies colonists had been gathering in Concord. On their way, they stopped on the green in front of a tavern in Lexington to face a group of minutemen. While each side claimed the other fired first, that mattered not. Of great significance was "the shot heard round the world" had settled the question of whether the conflict would be settled by words or war.

IX

Clinging to Loyalty While Striving to Protect Liberty

News of the April 19 battles at Lexington and Concord had barely percolated its way through all the colonies by the time the Second Continental Congress met in Philadelphia on May 10, 1775. Delegates had read information regarding the shots fired at Lexington and the battle at Concord. They also had read stories of Redcoats murdering unarmed men and women, and maliciously burning houses during their chaotic retreat. Those assaults had been described in the florid language of the day. No doubt many nodded with satisfaction when they learned the Redcoats had suffered almost 300 casualties, while the patriot losses were fewer than 100.[236]

One important change in the Second Continental Congress's makeup was the appearance of a Georgia delegate. Although the new delegate was there representing only the colony's St. John parish, a claim finally could be made that the Congress spoke for all thirteen mainland British colonies.[237]

Patriot delegates to the Second Congress who strongly favored a move to independence were pleased that the British now could be held responsible for initiating military action against them. But they kept their views within their own self-selected group.

Those who steadfastly maintained a goal of reaffiliation with the mother country were dismayed at the British military initiative, but held to a firm resolution in pursuing the defense of American rights. Leader of that group, John Dickinson, publicly expressed his sentiment and that of his ideological friends. He said that "this most unnatural and inexpressibly cruel war began with the butchery of the unarmed Americans." He added: "While we revere and love our mother country, her sword is opening our veins."[238]

And speaking of the mother country ...

In London, almost two months before the British assault on Lexington and Concord, Lord North tried another ploy to create divisions within the colonies. In late February, he introduced an "Olive Branch" resolution in Parliament. The resolution announced that any colony which stipulated it would levy taxes "for contributing their proportion to the common defence...and shall engage to make provision also for the support of the civil government, and the administration of justice," with the defense funds being forwarded to London, will receive a pledge from Parliament to not tax that colony's citizens, and will be received back into the empire. That was, provided Parliament thought the funds sent to London were adequate to the purpose.[239]

The opposition in Parliament ridiculed the proposal as being nothing but self-serving. Edmund Burke made one of the most scathing criticisms. Under the resolution, colonies would:

> be held in durance by troops, fleets, and armies, until singly and separately they shall do—what? Until they shall offer to contribute to a service which they cannot know, in a proportion which they cannot guess, on a standard which they are so far from being able to ascertain, that Parliament which is to hold it, has not ventured to hint what it is they expect.[240]

In truth, Burke and his fellow critics had it right. The day before North introduced the plan in the Commons he wrote King George III (referring to himself in the third person rather than the first person, which sometimes was used by individuals writing to the king to show deference to the king). He said that he expected the plan to be of:

> great utility (if not in America, at least on this side of the water) to arise to the public from this motion; he is confident it gives up no right, and that it contains precisely the plan which ought to be adopted by Great Britain, even if all America were subdued. He has reason to think it would give general satisfaction here, and that it will greatly facilitate passing the Bill now in the House.…

The latter was a bill to prohibit New England colonies from trading with any nation other than Britain, and blocking their fishermen from access to the Newfoundland banks. The king indicated his pleasure with the resolution because it would find favor in the Parliament and because the offer being made was to go to the individual colonies, ignoring the existence of the Continental Congress, which he considered an illegal body.[241]

After the resolution passed Parliament, Lord Dartmouth sent it to the governors in America. In those colonies that still had functioning "official" legislatures, members considered the resolution and rejected it, as Benjamin Franklin had forecast. He wrote to Joseph Galloway that the plan "holds a sword" over the head of colonial legislatures, and noted Prime Minister North wrote it in the "language of a highwayman."

Meanwhile, war had broken out, and defense was the word of the day in Philadelphia. Any military action patriot troops took must be limited to defense. The delegates stipulated: "this Congress has nothing more in view than the defense of the colonies." In this respect, delegates were placing reason over emotion, for up and down the colonies enthusiasm for resisting British force with American force was reaching a flash point. Men, young and old, organized themselves into militia units and prepared for action.[242]

Both Massachusetts and New York patriots pressed the Congress on related matters. Massachusetts leaders said an army was required to defend American liberties from British aggression. An "army" of militia troops had been set up around the entrance to the Boston peninsula as soon as British forces had fled back into Boston following the battle at Concord. Now, Massachusetts leaders wanted to see this force molded into a national fighting force. Congress tabled the proposal to authorize an army.

The New York message could not be put off easily. It asked what the patriots were to do if British troops arrived. Stressing they must limit themselves to defensive action, Congress told the New Yorkers that if British troops landed, they should be allowed to settle into available barracks, but to prevent the soldiers from building new fortifications. Only if the troops opened hostilities or attempted to confiscate private property should the patriots use military force.[243]

More important than the Congress's timidity in delaying a decision on forming an army and its weak-kneed response to New York's question was the fact leaders in the colonies were looking to that Congress as their parent. Indeed, in the weeks and months following these queries, one after another of the colonies asked Congress for advice or directions on important issues. While certainly not without disagreements, and sometimes internal clashes, volunteer colonial organizations were trying to work with the volunteer "national" Congress cooperatively. Many serious verbal challenges and some physical clashes were occurring in towns, cities, and counties, and some intercolonial conflicts were arising, but for a hodgepodge of voluntary, *ad hoc* organizations and associations facing uncertain threats, patriot-governing bodies were proving remarkably effective.

What made the transformation of governments all the more remarkable was the presence in local and some colony-wide organizations of men from the middle class who never before had held any responsible leadership post, except perhaps in their church. Yet all that striving for effective, responsible governance did not always mean smooth sailing in difficult situations.[244]

The Continental Congress's initial avoidance of a request to authorize an army left Massachusetts patriot leaders in a quandary. Militia units arrived and left the area adjacent to Boston daily. While Massachusetts General Artemas Ward supervised and gave direction to military preparations, he worked under the Massachusetts Committee of Safety's authority. Complicating the work was the presence of a substantial number of Connecticut, Rhode Island, and New Hampshire troops. Though Connecticut military leaders placed themselves under Ward's command, and the other colonials deferred to him, clashes of opinion between rank-and-file soldiers from different colonies, sometimes expressed in violent outbursts, demonstrated the need for stronger troop management. But that could only transpire when Congress accepted and dealt with reality.[245]

One matter with which Congress was literally incapable of handling was restraining military initiative, since communication between the Massachusetts patriots' Cambridge military headquarters and Philadelphia took about a week each way. Another was that the Massachusetts Committee of Safety saw its job as defending its colony, and doing so meant those actually involved in that defense had to make decisions. So, when two proposals came to the Committee of Safety to send detachments to Fort Ticonderoga, located at the south end of Lake Champlain, to capture British cannon and provide a defensive shield against a possible British-Canadian assault, the committee authorized both missions. The result was an easy, noncombat transfer of power from British troops to American militia at Ticonderoga, although it was accompanied by a rash of personality and intercolonial jurisdictional disputes.

Congress had those disputes dumped in its lap.[246]

But only "defensive" military action was to be permitted. How could the capture of a British fort be deemed a defensive move? Filled, as Congress was, with experienced politicians, such a rationale flowed forth.

Taking the fort was a preemptive defensive action to prevent a British force from moving down Lake Champlain from Canada and using the fort as a staging area for wider assaults on America. Then, irrationally, Congress ordered the cannon at the fort to be moved to the south end of Lake George, leaving the fort defenseless. (Ticonderoga was located on a strip of land separating Lake Champlain to the east, and Lake George to the south.)

Congress ordered an inventory taken of all military equipment at the fort so "that they may be safely returned when the restoration of the former harmony between Great Britain and these colonies so ardently wished for by the latter shall render it prudent."[247]

When a rumor came to Philadelphia that a joint British-Indian force was headed to retake Fort Ticonderoga, Congress reversed itself and directed the cannons remain at the fort. That settled one matter. Domestically, though, disputes continued because the fort was located within New York. The Massachusetts patriots had not consulted the provincial New York government before authorizing the fort's capture. Furthermore, one of the officers involved in the capture had a hundred dollar bounty on his head from New York for his actions in opposing New York settlers trying to move into an area (now known as Vermont) which both New York and New Hampshire claimed. Eventually the conflicts were resolved. Congress used the episode as an opportunity to send messages to Canadians that it sympathized with them for the tyranny they were suffering under the dictates of the Quebec Act.[248]

Another challenge Congress had to address was a recommendation that, with Fort Ticonderoga in hand, plans should be developed to invade Canada, since the only British force there was a small garrison of Redcoats. Insisting it was only interested in furthering defensive measures until the British government agreed to honor American demands for reunification, Congress rejected the invasion proposal. Amazingly, less than a month later it authorized an invasion of Canada. But between those two dates, a second major battle was fought: the "Battle of Bunker Hill."[249]

Near the end of May additional British troops arrived in Boston. General Gage received three major generals to assist him, along with a new set of orders. The orders told Gage he was to exercise initiative in destroying colonial munitions and also break out from his cramped confinement in Boston.

Gage and his trio of generals decided to occupy two sets of hills that commanded Boston and, after their capture, assault the main patriot force. The two targets were the hills on the Charlestown peninsula, immediately to the north of Boston, and Dorchester heights, on a peninsula just to the southwest of the city. Before he could complete planning these actions, spies passed along Gage's plans to patriot headquarters in Cambridge. General Ward ordered troops to go on to the Charlestown peninsula and build fortifications on Bunker Hill in an overnight move. Finding Breed's Hill more suitable for the purpose, the men threw up breastworks there.[250]

General Ward had fashioned a foolish plan. Charlestown, location of the two hills, Bunker and Breed, was a peninsula, with only a narrow neck connecting it to the mainland. All the British had to do was occupy the neck and then destroy the American troops, who would have no means of either resupply or escape. But such tactics would not get General Gage the glory he wanted.

Gage decided to attack the American forces, numbering somewhere between 1,500 and 2,000 men, with a frontal assault. To accomplish this glorious victory, he had about 2,200 Redcoats make the attack. Twice, the colonial defenders stopped the assaulting British, inflicting heavy casualties each time. During the third Redcoat attack, the Americans ran out of powder and retreated, leaving the field to the British. Gage claimed a great victory. Patriots, and the North administration in London thought otherwise.

Yes, General Gage's men took Charlestown, but at the cost of over 1,000 casualties—nearly 50 percent of the attacking force— while the American "rabble," so called by some British political leaders, suffered a loss of about 450 men. As one member of the

North administration wryly noted: "We certainly are victorious in this engagement of the 17th, but if we have eight more such victories there will be nobody left to bring news of them... ." That ended Gage's plan to break out of Boston and then attack the main American army. A short time later, General Lord Howe replaced General Gage as commander of British troops in America. Gage's military career in America, stretching back over two decades, came to an ignominious end.[251]

While military activity in Massachusetts was moving to a horrific clash of arms, members of Congress were busy taking themselves and the colonies down two seemingly contradictory paths. To those still loyal to Britain and passionately dedicated to restoring cooperative relations with the mother country, Congress authorized yet another "humble" petition to the king, expressing Americans' continued fealty to him, and seeking his help in restoring the colonies to their proper place in the king's empire.[252]

Recognizing the hope for peaceful settlement of differences was slim, Congress also adopted practical measures to promote colonial defenses. It authorized the purchase of gunpowder, ordered companies of riflemen from Virginia, Maryland, and Pennsylvania to march to Massachusetts, the men to be paid from Congressional funds. Congress then made the implication it was creating an army official. On June 14, 1775, it adopted the militia units facing the British army in Boston as a Continental force. It selected George Washington to become General of the Continental Army. Congress also appointed a committee to draft a statement for General Washington to read to the troops, explaining why those troops were, in fact, facing the British army.[253]

Creating an effective civil government was a continuing bone of contention in war-torn Massachusetts. Popularly elected local committees and a provincial congress were hard at work, but they functioned without any "constitutional" authority. The Massachusetts provincial congress twice asked the Continental Congress for advice before the latter offered suggestions.

Congress equivocated. Massachusetts should ignore Parliament's 1774 alteration of its charter. The provincial congress should organize a new government based as close as possible on the 1691 charter. Accordingly, the Congress told the Massachusetts provincial congress it should call for elections in all districts claiming representation in the former assembly. Once the new assembly met, it was to elect an upper house/council. The two bodies should jointly rule the colony until the king's government appointed a new governor who was willing to govern under the principles of the unamended 1691 charter. Some in Massachusetts cheered the advice; others complained that what they needed was a new frame of government respecting citizens' right to rule themselves.

Modest as the Continental Congress's advice was, it marked another step away from dependency on Britain and toward independence. In 1774, Congress had refused to suggest how colonial governance should be organized. Now, in mid-1775, Congress offered such advice. Yet members would not be rushed. Congress rejected proposals to advise colonies to open American ports to international shipping.[254]

Delegates to the Continental Congress took their responsibilities very seriously. They struggled to balance their own views with delegates holding different positions. The narrative to this point shows some of the difficulties delegates had in meeting each other halfway when framing policies. These difficulties came forth again when delegates considered two different documents: a petition to the king, and a statement explaining why colonists were resisting British military force.

John Dickinson wrote the petition to the king. Congress also assigned Dickinson and Thomas Jefferson to collaborate on the statement to be read to the troops mounting the defensive bastions against British military assaults.

In the petition to King George III, Dickinson gave a classic rationale when appealing to monarchs: the populace loved the king, but his evil advisors were corrupting the government. British statutes causing oppression to loyal American colonists must be repealed. American military resistance to British assaults did not imply disrespect to the king, but a determination to resist tyranny.

Dickinson's petition, labeled the "Olive Branch Petition," as was true of those preceding it, made clear that while colonists maintained loyalty to the Crown, they would offer no concessions. Having written as moderate a request as he thought he could, Dickinson said the petition offered nothing new. Rather, in the likely event the king rejected it, that rejection "will confirm the minds of our countrymen to endure all the misfortunes that may attend the contest." So, while hoping the king might—just might—have a change of heart, Dickinson recognized the greater likelihood was that the petition would help domestically to steel men and women to persevere in defense of liberty. Even so, he or one of his likeminded colleagues took another step in trying to catch a sympathetic royal ear. A member of the Penn family, which continued as proprietors of Pennsylvania, was persuaded to carry the "Olive Branch Petition" personally to London.[255]

Wanting this final plea for British understanding to stand out upon its receipt in England, when the Congress heard that the New Jersey legislature also was planning a petition to the king, a three-member delegation, which Dickinson headed, and including a prominent New York moderate, left Philadelphia for nearby Burlington, New Jersey to confer with that colony's assembly. After listening to the three Continental Congress delegates for about an hour, members of the assembly voted to table the motion to send a petition to the king until they received word concerning the reception given the Congressional petition in London. Thus, Congress prevented any thought in England that a division of sentiment separated the colonies from the Congress.[256]

As far as the second writing project went, Dickinson's draft of the "Declaration of the Causes and Necessity of Taking up Arms" was anything but mild and submissive. Indeed, despite his passionate desire to see a peaceful settlement between Britain and the colonies, Dickinson spoke stridently in the document—

though not as stridently as Jefferson did in his version of the statement, which he ultimately held back, in order to maintain at least technical "unity" within the Congress.

Dickinson combined condemnation of evil ministers imposing tyrannical measures on colonists with those same colonists' devotion to long-cherished freedoms for which they now were prepared to fight and die. Even so, he still maintained that the colonists wanted nothing more than to rejoin the British Empire on happy terms. Invoking God's support, he said the colonists "implore his divine goodness to protect us through this great conflict, to dispose our adversaries to reconciliation on reasonable terms, and therefore to relieve the empire of the calamities of civil war." Near the conclusion, Dickinson presented statements as fact which either were not yet true or were based on hope: "Our Cause is just. Our Union is perfect. Our preparations nearly complete. Our internal Resources are great; and our Assurance of Foreign Aid is certain."

There could hardly be a perfect union when the Continental Congress itself had no written framework or rationale as a basis for its proceedings, and individual colonies still were seeking guidance from the Congress concerning the creation of formal governmental structures. In terms of receiving foreign aid, the Congress had not yet sought such assistance.[257]

As in so many declarations during the tension-filled days between the Boston Tea Party and the colonies' final break with Britain, this one, to be read to the troops as well as shared with all the colonists and even sent to England, mixed fact, fiction, and hope with the expectation such a combination would elicit faith in "the cause" by Americans and concern about the ultimate outcome by those in England.

Those still dedicated to a return to cordial relations between Britain and the colonies, both in Congress and in the colonies, had ample reason to worry about how the king would receive the "Olive Branch Petition." When Richard Penn reached London in August 1775, he conferred with Arthur Lee, who still served as the Massachusetts representative in London, as well as others who had been colonial agents. Only Lee was willing to join Penn in submitting the petition to Lord Dartmouth, still serving as Secretary for America. After overcoming some difficulties, the two men got the petition to Dartmouth. They pressed him for information on how the king might react. Dartmouth told them *"no answer would be given."* After this harsh rejection, Penn and Lee distributed copies of the petition to the London press, and it became a matter of public discussion.[258]

The story did not end there. The Duke of Grafton, who for several years had been serving as Lord Privy Seal, wrote to Lord North, pleading with him to give the petition serious consideration as the last possible hope for bringing the colonies back into the empire without further military conflict. Grafton later wrote in his memoirs that:

> It was evident to all considerate men, that the connection of the two countries hung on the decision; for it was stated to many that on the vote for Independence, Mr. Dickinson and his party had the ascendancy in favour of dependence on this country: and besides, it was equally well known, that a compromise had taken place in order to render the petition unanimous....

Both the king and Lord North already had made their decisions. The colonies would be reunited with the mother country through force of arms. North waited five weeks to inform the Duke that compromise with the colonies was no longer under consideration.[259]

When Parliament returned from its summer vacation on October 26, the king gave both members of the Commons and the Lords his interpretation of the petition. "The Authors and promoters of this desperate Conspiracy have meant only to amuse by vague Expressions of Attachment to the Parent State, and the strongest Protestations of Loyalty to Me, while they were preparing for a General Revolt." That sounded like a complete rejection of the "Olive Branch," and preparation for all-out war.[260]

But, wait a minute…

A proposal Lord Dartmouth had made some months earlier, only to have the king dismiss it, still gave Lord North hope negotiations could shorten the conflict. Dartmouth had advocated sending a peace delegation to the colonies with authority to grant pardons to contrite colonists and return whole colonies to favored positions within the empire when their leadership agreed to subservience to Parliament. Lord North brought this plan forth and, while his cabinet officers arranged for General Howe's military reinforcements, he conducted a prolonged series of conferences and discussions on the peace commission idea. He decided to send Admiral Lord Howe, brother of General Howe, as the principal negotiator. Admiral Howe had many contacts with leading colonials and was well liked by them. But the slow pace at which the plan moved conveyed the impression that sending the mission to confer with the colonists was not urgent, for more than six months elapsed between North's initial proposals and the mission's implementation. By the time Lord Howe arrived in America, the "colonists" were no more. They were Americans.[261]

X

Choosing Liberty over Loyalty

As King George III, Lord North, and Lord Dartmouth considered Britain's relations with its American colonies in 1775, they all seemed to forget that "loyalty" is a value, not a behavioral trait. Individuals gain the loyalty of others by earning it; they cannot command it. Those in charge may be able to order obedience from those they "control," but they must earn loyalty. Effective leaders, be they military commanders, corporate officers, government officials, or heads of volunteer groups, understand the difference and behave accordingly. Egotistical autocrats think of obedience and loyalty as synonyms, and are infuriated when they "demand" loyalty and receive only grudging obedience.

King George III made clear he did not understand the meaning of "loyalty" when he told Lord North he wanted to "drive them [the colonists] into submission." Lord North and his cabinet officers seemed to think along like paths.

In October 1775, the British naval commander for the colonies ordered an eight-gun ship and a smaller schooner to sail north from Boston and destroy towns along the coast. The detachment commander cruised past Gloucester, Massachusetts because the houses visible from the water were too far apart to burn easily. He took his pair of vessels on up the coast until he reached Falmouth. (Falmouth is now Portland, Maine.) Facing virtually no opposition there, he gave the townspeople notice he intended to destroy their homes and public buildings. Some brave citizens negotiated with the commander and gained time to evacuate. The next morning, using cannon and incendiaries, along with hand-carried torches, the British burned some two hundred private homes, plus the church, library, other public buildings, wharves, and several boats. Apparently deciding Falmouth's destruction satisfied the orders he had received, the commander returned to Boston.[262]

To the south, military conflicts also were under way. In April and May 1775, Lord Dunmore, British governor of Virginia, engaged in mostly verbal battles with the colonists. His troops did capture a store of powder in Williamsburg, only to have the governor pay for it in order to avoid a fight with an angry militia force descending on the town. Shortly after this, Dunmore abandoned the governor's mansion in the dark of night and took refuge on a British warship at Yorktown.[263]

Dunmore schemed with others to bring the wrath of Indians against the Virginians, but alert colonists captured his agents before they reached the tribes in the Ohio valley. Dunmore also conspired to create a loyalist force as well as an "Ethiopian" troop of runaway slaves for whom he promised freedom in exchange for fighting on the British side. (When colonists forced Dunmore and the fleet to flee in the spring of 1776, Dunmore shipped many of the escaped slaves to the British West Indies, where they were sold back into slavery.)[264]

Lord Dunmore's final assault on Virginia began on the morning of January 1, 1776. He had the ships in his command fire on the port town of Norfolk, the principal seaport for exporting tobacco to Britain. Continuing for seven hours, the bombardment, coupled with landing parties that spread incendiaries, leveled 80 percent of the town. Patriot leaders then took over the job and destroyed the few standing buildings so they could not be used to shelter enemy forces.[265]

The two naval assaults on port towns, north and south, along with pitched battles in Massachusetts and elsewhere, and the threat of new Indian raids no doubt did, as the British hoped, spread fear—perhaps even terror—throughout the colonies. They also stimulated another emotion. The assaults and threatened assaults, when coupled with news from England that the king had signed a "Proclamation of Rebellion," and that Britain intended to have thousands of foreign "Hessian" troops fight in America, generated waves of anger and a fresh look at the idea of American independence. (In fact, the British government signed treaties with two Germanic principalities for a total of 12,500 mercenary troops, the larger force coming from the Langrave of Hesse-Cassel, hence "Hessian" troops.)[266]

Giving a significant boost to this renewed look at independence was the publication of the most electrifying and influential pamphlet of its time: "Common Sense." A Philadelphia printer initially published "Common Sense" anonymously in January 1776 It sold at least 120,000 copies by March, and tens of thousands more went out in succeeding weeks.[267]

Arriving in Philadelphia from London in 1774, thirty-eight-year-old Thomas Pain [Paine] carried with him letters of introduction from Benjamin Franklin which first landed him work as a teacher. Before long he changed his focus and was writing articles for a local publication. All the while, he found himself caught up in discussions regarding the colonies' current and future status. Though raised a Quaker, Pain had moved away from that denomination, and to deism during his difficult young adult years when he often changed jobs, twice failed in business and once in marriage. Finally he resolved to make a new start in a distant land.

Moving from place to place in England, Pain encountered politically oriented men with whom he either shared or argued ideas. As he did so, he shaped his own ideas of government and society, and in those ideas there was no room for monarchy.[268]

Having brought some firmly held political views with him when he sailed to America, he developed new ideas in his new country. During the 1775 fall and winter, he wrote a pamphlet that he had published in January 1776 as "Common Sense." The first edition listed no author, but rather the statement: "written by an Englishman."

Eventually, he revealed himself as the author, but with a change in his name. Now considering himself an American rather than an Englishman, Pain added a letter to his last name: Paine.[269]

In his introduction, Paine gave the conflict between Britain and America a universal context: "The cause of America is in a great measure the cause of all mankind." Next, the author made clear his view of government as an institution, and it was not pretty:

> Society in every state is a blessing, but government even in its best state is but a necessary evil; in its worst state an intolerable one; for when we suffer, or are exposed to the same miseries by a government, which we might expect in a country without government, our calamities is heightened by reflecting that we furnish the means by which we suffer.[270]

What might be the source of such "calamities" Paine asked his readers. Showing that his personal travels from Quakerism to deism had not left him bereft of biblical knowledge, he began his new thrust with forays into the Old Testament. "Monarchy is ranked in scripture as one of the sins of the Jews, for which a curse in reserve is denounced against them." He then recounted stories of Gideon and Samuel from the Old Testament to validate his claim, concluding: "WE HAVE ADDED UNTO OUR SINS THIS EVIL, TO ASK A KING."

Next came a condemnation of hereditary transfer of monarchical power, concluding his analysis with the devastating statement: "Of more worth is one honest man to society, and in the sight of God, than all the Crowned ruffians that ever lived."[271]

Warning those still devoted to returning the colonies to dependency within Great Britain what would befall them, Paine focused on the king's power.

The powers of governing still remaining in the hands of the k—, he will have a negative over the whole legislation of this continent. And as he hath shewn himself such an inveterate enemy to liberty, and discovered such a thirst for arbitrary power; is he, or is he not, a proper man to say to these colonies, "you shall make no laws but what I please."[272]

Large families were the norm in America, and Paine appealed to parental responsibility, using the unstated fact that Britain was still struggling with a massive debt accumulated during the Seven Years' War. Possibly the British government would transfer requirements for paying down part of that debt to American colonies, were those colonies to again become subjects of Britain:

As parents, we can have no joy, knowing that this government is not sufficiently lasting to ensure any thing which we may bequeath to posterity: And by a plain method of argument, as we are running the next generation into debt, we ought to do the work of it, otherwise we use them meanly and pitifully. In order to discover the line of our duty rightly, we should take our children in our hand, and fix our station a few years farther into life; that eminence will present a prospect, which a few present fears and prejudices conceal from our sight.

With these and other arguments, facts, logic, and emotional outpourings, a few of which were either inaccurate or strained, Paine drove home the idea that independence would come to America sooner or later, and the propitious time was now. Appealing to homegrown pride, he reminded his readers that: "there is something very absurd, in supposing a continent to be perpetually governed by an island."[273]

Paine did not just write of the essential need for independence. He lived the part, joining the Continental Army in July 1776.

Reaction to "Common Sense" was close to instantaneous, given the speed of communication then. After reading it, some Congressmen sent copies home, hoping those reading it would join the call for independence. One Congressman reported hearing that in Pennsylvania, where the provincial assembly had declared against independence, after reading the pamphlet, a heavy majority of citizens "are now full in his Sentiments; in the Jerseys & Maryland &c they gain ground daily." A North Carolina Congressman went home, and along the way he "heard nothing praised in the Course of his Journey but Common sense and Independence."[274]

After reading it, General Washington wrote a correspondent that "the sound doctrine and unanswerable reasoning contained in the pamphlet Common Sense, will not leave numbers at a loss to decide upon the propriety of a separation." Washington's officers also were reading it. A chaplain to a Connecticut regiment had dinner with several others on March 4, 1776, the night their troops went on to Dorchester Heights to fortify it. He dined with a general officer, two colonels, a captain, and another chaplain. Later he wrote in his diary: "The topicks of conversation; the designed maneuvers at Dorchester... Remarks on Common Sense; immediate independency of Great Britain &c."[275]

Reading "Common Sense" and approving its sentiment and its arguments did not, of themselves, catapult patriots into a paroxysm of revolutionary zeal. As the foremost historian of ideas during the Revolutionary Era has noted, "Common Sense":

> did not touch off the movement for a formal declaration of independence, and it did not create the Revolutionary leaders' determination to build a better world, more open to humane aspirations, than had ever been known before. But it stimulated both....[276]

Of course, any meaningful move for independence remained in the hands of the assembled Continental Congress. There, disagreements between advocates of separation and those maintaining a shred of hope for reconciliation sometimes turned from treating colleagues with "decency and respect," as one Congressman noted, to: "Jealousies, ill natured observations and recriminations," which "take [the] place of reason and Argument... ."[277]

Representatives to the Congress had been selected, in most cases, by their colony's provincial assembly. Most of those assemblies sent the chosen delegates off to Philadelphia with instructions as to how they should vote if the question of independence arose. Several of those instructions specified their representatives to Congress should vote against independence. Would sentiment against independence among members of colonial assemblies change after first learning the British were burning whole towns, and then reading the inflammatory pamphlet? Were these issues enough to change the minds of those still adhering to subservience toward the Crown, so they sought, instead, liberty for the colonists? Many in Philadelphia had that question on their minds during the first months of 1776.

Momentum for change began at the local level, and gradually spread across individual colonies. Yet most colonial assemblies were reluctant to declare the old British rule in their colony was canceled without Congressional approval. Members of Congress understood the deference those colonial bodies were giving it—a deference colonial legislatures had not given Parliament in recent years.

Congress took a bold move toward independence on April 6, 1776, when it opened colonial ports to international trade. Then in early May 1776, Congress took up "the state of the United Colonies." Emerging from a three-day discussion and debate on the subject in the committee of the whole, Congress unanimously adopted a resolution calling for the colonies to create legitimate new governments, telling the *ad hoc* legislators: where no government sufficient to the exigencies of their affairs have been hitherto established," they should create "such government as shall... best conduce to the happiness and safety of their constituents in particular, and America in general." So, Congress reciprocated on the deference colonial assemblies had been giving to it. The resolution gave those assemblies full leeway to prepare a frame of government for their residents without placing any constraints on the work, other than to say the framework should promote "the happiness and safety" of their citizens.[278]

Deciding the resolution needed a preamble, Congress appointed a three-member committee to prepare one: Edward Rutledge, Richard Henry Lee, and John Adams. The first two chose John Adams to write it. He did.

This preamble became significant in the course of the year because it changed the nature of colonists' opposition to Britain. Adams began the preamble with what was at the time a shocking statement: "Whereas his Britannic Majesty, in conjunction with the lords and commons of Great Britain has, by a late act of Parliament, excluded the inhabitants of these United Colonies from the protection of the Crown...." The shock was that Adams attacked the king directly: "his Britannic Majesty." In previous petitions and resolutions, colonists attacked Parliament or the king's "evil" ministers, while professing continued loyalty to the monarch. This time, the monarchy was the first institution attacked. It was coupled with Parliament as being responsible for the break between colonies and Britain. Such a statement was a necessary prelude to announcing a complete break with the British government, and John Adams was ready to make the announcement. Not surprisingly, the preamble did not stop there, but also stipulated that "it is necessary that the exercise of every kind of authority under the said crown should be totally suppressed, and all the powers of government exerted, under the authority of the people of the colonies...."[279]

In all probability, John Locke's "Second Treatise on Government" inspired John Adams to attack the king directly. Adams had this essay in his personal library. Locke explained the difference between resistance to government and revolution within the context of English law and history. The difference centered with the king. If one protested against actions the king's ministers took, one was attacking policies those evil ministers formulated. The king, who was, in effect, the government, stood above the fray. "He can do no Wrong himself...." But if the king, as a "magistrate," acts unlawfully, he ceases to hold his exalted position "and acting without Authority, may be opposed..." as a private person. Of course, as a "private person" he has no special standing in law.[280]

Reaction in Congress to Adams's statement was swift and critical; the debate heated. A New York Congressman said his instructions did not allow him to vote for such a sweeping statement. Others complained the preamble made void the existing colonial assemblies. They, it turned out, were in the minority. In an unrecorded vote, privately noted as either six to four, or perhaps seven to four states, with two or one states abstaining, the Continental Congress adopted the preamble.[281]

Though John Adams and others thought his statement in fact separated the colonies from Britain, Adams acknowledged that a formal declaration to that effect still was required. Others, inside Congress and in some of the colonies, had similar thoughts.

Southern colonial assemblies led the way in supporting a continental declaration of independence, with North Carolina having the honor of initiating this movement among the colonies. It gave specific instructions to its Continental Congressmen to support "declaring independency and forming foreign alliances." South Carolina and Georgia simply gave their Congressmen discretion to vote for whatever motions or resolutions they thought would protect or promote the interests of their colony.[282]

When the Virginia convention reconvened in May 1776, delegates were inundated with resolutions, petitions, and letters from all parts of the colony calling for independence—another sign of local initiatives influencing colony (soon to be state) policy decisions. Convention delegates followed the wishes of those who had contacted them. They instructed their delegates in Congress: "to propose to that respectable body to declare the United Colonies free and independent States, absolved from all allegiance to, or dependence upon, the Crown or Parliament of Great Britain...." The directions came with a self-defense proviso: "That the power of forming Government and the regulation of the internal concerns of each Colony, be left to the respective Colonial Legislatures." The Virginia convention sent the resolution not only to its members in Congress, but also to the other colonies.[283]

The Virginia convention's major task that May was to create a state constitution. Through diligent work and a cooperative attitude among the delegates, it accomplished this in relatively short order. But delegates thought that before approving the document, they should announce to the world that Virginia was no longer part of the British Empire. The new state constitution began with a preamble that stated that because King George III had attempted to impose on the people of Virginia a "detestable and insupportable Tyranny," the colony's ties to Great Britain were "totally dissolved." Here is another bow to John Locke's idea concerning the root cause of revolution: the king, as tyrant, had lost any claim to be recognized as ruler. Now, at least one new state preceded the Continental Congress in declaring independence from Great Britain.[284]

On June 7, 1776, Virginia Congressman Richard Henry Lee proposed to his colleagues:

> That these United Colonies are, and of right ought to be, free and independent States, that they are absolved from all allegiance to the British Crown, and that all political connection between them and the State of Great Britain is, and ought to be, totally dissolved.[285]

Knowing that the king's ministers had tried various ways to divide the colonies in order to weaken American resistance, Congressional leaders believed the pronouncement of independence should be supported with not just a majority of colonies, but as close as possible to unanimity. Because of this, Lee and his close allies, the Adams cousins, were willing to delay a vote on Lee's motion in hopes those colonies that had instructed their representatives in Congress to oppose independence would have a change of heart.

Congressmen debated the proposal for three days, and on June 10 decided to delay a vote on it until July 1. Yet anticipating a favorable vote at that time, the following day, June 11, Congress authorized a committee of five to draft a declaration of independence. Foremost on the committee were Thomas Jefferson, Benjamin Franklin, and John Adams, although when they met, they gave Jefferson the assignment of preparing the initial draft.[286]

Richard Henry Lee's motion for independence also included statements calling for a formal confederation of the independent colonies, and the formation of alliances with foreign powers. Toward those ends, Congress appointed a committee to draft a frame of union and a committee to formulate treaty documents.

(Looking forward, the committee assigned to prepare treaty documents had the easier time, for a treaty with France was signed two years later. Those on the committee to prepare a constitution must have experienced prolonged periods of frustration, for the Articles of Confederation were not finalized and ratified for five years. Quite a contrast with Virginia's drafting a constitution in a few weeks.)

With only three weeks to change several colonial assemblies' position against independence, swift action was necessary. Strategically important colonies had not yet authorized their representatives to vote for independence. In fact, the entire middle of the thirteen colonies had resisted the call for independence: Maryland, Delaware, Pennsylvania, New Jersey, and New York. Fortunately, all were within a day's travel from Philadelphia.[287]

The reluctant colonial provisional assemblies found themselves pressured from both their local constituents and from members of the Continental Congress to accept what in fact, if not in theory, existed. Britain had formally removed the colonies from its dominion, and a fighting war for independence was under way, even if no military action had yet taken place in those colonies' population centers. Local communities, county associations, and voluntary organizations were expressing themselves in favor of independence. The ground swell of local initiatives must have pressured delegates in provisional assemblies to rethink their dreams of retaining ties to Mother England.

In June several Maryland counties called for their delegates in the provincial Convention to advocate independence. One of them, Charles County, in southern Maryland, which knew it was vulnerable to amphibious British attacks from both the Chesapeake Bay and the Potomac River, told its five delegates to the provincial Convention to work for a declaration of independence in the Continental Congress. In a lengthy statement members of the county excoriated the British king and government, warned that an invasion by British troops was imminent, and pled for swift action to bring unity to the colonies because:

> we are convinced that nothing virtuous, humane, generous, or just, can be expected from the British king or nation, and that they will exert themselves to reduce us to a state of slavery, by every effort and artifice in their power, [therefore] we are of opinion that the time has fully arrived for the Colonies to adopt the last measure for our common good and safety, and that the sooner they declare themselves separate from, and independent of the Crown and Parliament of Great Britain, the sooner they will be able to make effectual opposition, and establish their liberties on a firm and permanent basis.[288]

Five military battalions in Pennsylvania did likewise. Two New York towns, in addition to "private" organizations such as the Mechanics, added their call for independence.

Although Massachusetts already was firmly in support of independence, town after town in that colony wished it known they were behind the movement. In fact, no fewer than fifty-five towns adopted formal resolutions committing their residents to support independence. Many of these statements recounted injustices suffered under actions of the king and Parliament, mostly in the very recent past. A few issued statements that were short and to the point, such as the town of Ashby, Massachusetts. Its terse statement said the assembled inhabitants of the town "unanimously voted as follows, viz: That should the honourable Congress, for the safety of the Colonies, declare them independent of Great Britain, the inhabitants of Ashby will solemnly engage with their lives and fortunes to support them in the measure."[289]

One Massachusetts town, Barnstable, on Cape Cod, in a close vote, stood out for opposing independence.

The number of communities and organizations calling for independence did not necessarily influence provisional legislatures as much as the passion flowing from the statements those communities sent forward. For example, the resolution adopted in Frederick County, Maryland—one of the colony's western counties—chastised timid legislators. Keeping Maryland from joining the majority of colonies in favoring independence was "destructive to our internal safety, and big with publick ruin." Members of the Chester County militia told the Pennsylvania legislators that isolating Pennsylvania from other colonies on the question of independence was "calculated to break an important middle link in the grand Continental chain of Union."[290]

One by one, provincial legislatures in the hesitant colonies changed their position on independence. Delaware was the first, on June 15. New Jersey followed a week later. In short order, Pennsylvania followed. Then came Maryland on June 28. Later it added a formal "Declaration" on July 6. This left only New York. It held back until Congress acted. Then, on July 9, it released its members of Congress to sign the document.[291]

Having received instructions from the Continental Congress on June 11 to draft a statement on independence, the four other committee members turned to Thomas Jefferson to prepare it. Upon completing it, Jefferson showed his draft to both Adams and Franklin. Each of them made minor literary alterations. Jefferson then prepared a clean copy for the entire committee to consider. After it did so, he submitted it to the Congress, which, following the vote for independence on July 2, debated and made several changes to Jefferson's draft, finally approving it on July 4.[292]

For some years, as far back as 1765 with the Stamp Act Congress, petitions had been sent to Parliament pleading for a redress of colonial grievances. Individual colonies followed suit in subsequent years. But by the time the first Continental Congress met, many in America had rejected the idea that the colonies fell under parliamentary control and instead denied that Parliament could legislate for the colonies. Rather, they claimed allegiance to Britain only through a compact with the Crown. In part, this flowed from changing views on political philosophy, giving increasing importance to "natural law," in which individuals formed themselves into voluntary associations for mutual security and protection of their liberties, "voluntarily" ceding legal authority to a central government or ruler, in this case the Crown.

In part, the shift to a narrow allegiance to the Monarchy came from a negative or defensive view that Parliament was determined to dominate the colonies and make them completely subservient to its will. This flowed from laws Parliament passed, such as the Currency Act, which prevented colonies from creating paper currency backed by colonial taxes, the Quartering Act of 1765, and the Townshend Duties. It also was based in part on the British government's veto of colonial legislation, such as provisions to grant legislative representation to newly formed western counties in several colonies. But the solid base of the defensive shift away from colonial recognition of Parliament in favor of acknowledging King George III as the only legitimate political tie between colonies and mother country was the Declaratory Act of 1766, in which Parliament stated unequivocally that it had authority to rule the colonies "in all cases whatsoever." Yet a biographer of King George III said of the law, it was "an Act declaratory of the sovereign power of king and parliament over the colonies in all matters." This indicated the king was complicit in all parliamentary acts.[293]

Both the first and second Continental Congresses sent petitions to the king, asking him to defend the colonies against the tyrannical policies his government committed, which, of course, the petitions said were acting against the king's benevolent attitude toward the colonies. Yet more than a year before the second, "Olive Branch" petition reached London, some American leaders were drafting statements attacking the king. The most prominent was Thomas Jefferson's "Summary View of the Rights of British America", written in the summer of 1774. In it, Jefferson attacked the king directly, charging him with more than half a dozen actions violating American rights. Later, John Adams took up the cudgel in his preface to Congress's directions to the individual colonies to form new governments. At local levels, some colonies, counties, and towns prepared declarations in which they placed the reasons for separating from Great Britain at least in part on the king. In doing so, they often said they were declaring their independence to protect their liberty or freedom, which they were in danger of losing to Britain's tyrannical action.

Given these precedents, and the political ideology of the time, in the Declaration of Independence Jefferson quite properly attacked the king directly as the authority responsible for forcing the colonies to separate from Britain. Beginning with a generalization, Jefferson charged: "The history of the present king of Great Britain is a history of repeated injuries and usurpations, all having in direct object the establishment of an absolute Tyranny over these States." He then listed over thirty charges against the king, most of which involved either acts of Parliament that the king signed into law, or policies one of the Crown's administrative boards enforced, such as the Board of Trade or the Privy Council. A few were indirectly connected with the Crown through appointed colonial governors. An obvious example of parliamentary action was: "imposing Taxes upon us without our Consent." The Board of Trade had, on a number of occasions, "refused his Assent to Laws, the most wholesome and necessary for the public good." A North Carolina governor had deliberately sought to gain an advantage over a faction in the colony's legislature by calling "together legislative bodies at places unusual, uncomfortable, and distant from the depository of their public Records, for the sole purpose of fatiguing them into compliance with his measures." Then, too, the Massachusetts Government Act moved that colony's legislature from Boston to Salem. Yet even more terrifying charges were: "He has kept among us, in times of peace, Standing Armies without the Consent of our legislatures—He has affected to render the Military independent of and superior to the Civil power."[294]

Jefferson brought the charges against the king up to the moment:

> He has abdicated government here, by declaring us out of his Protection and waging War against us. — He has plundered our seas, ravaged our Coast, burnt our towns, and destroyed the lives of our people. — He is at this time transporting large Armies of foreign Mercenaries to compleat the works of death, desolation and tyranny, already begun with circumstances of Cruelty & perfidy scarcely paralleled in the most barbarous ages, and totally unworthy [of] the Head of a civilized nation.[295]

Stating what to Jefferson and his colleagues was obvious, "A Prince whose character is thus marked by every act which may define a Tyrant, is unfit to be the ruler of a free people." Because of these continuing assaults on American liberties,

> We, therefore, the Representatives of the united States of America, in General Congress, Assembled, appealing to the Supreme Judge of the world for the rectitude of our intentions do, in the Name, and by Authority of the good People of these Colonies, solemnly publish and declare, That these United Colonies are, and of Right ought to be Free and Independent States....[296]

Those signing the document also agreed that "for the support of this Declaration, with a firm reliance on the protection of divine Providence, we mutually pledge to each other our Lives, our Fortunes and our sacred Honor."[297]

Fifty-six members of Congress signed the Declaration, though securing all the signatures took some months. A few Congressmen, including John Dickinson of Pennsylvania, refused to sign. This did not mean they opposed the revolution, but they had not yet accepted in their own minds the necessity of making such a formal break with Britain. At the time, Dickinson was chairing the committee appointed to write America's first constitution, the Articles of Confederation.

Congress ordered copies of the document printed and forwarded to military units as well as state legislatures. The first public notice of the Declaration came two days after Congress adopted it, when the Pennsylvania Evening Post printed it on Saturday, July 6. Other newspapers followed suit as quickly as they could, usually placing it on the front page, with no editorial commentary. Celebrations followed. In Philadelphia, the Declaration was read from the State House at noon on Monday, July 8, in the presence of "many thousand." That was followed by a military parade and the ringing of church bells, some of which continued ringing into the night. Washington saw that the Declaration was read to every brigade in his army on July 10.[298]

The euphoria was short lived. Declaring independence was a promise (perhaps, even, simply a hope). Delivering independence was to cost thousands of lives, entail incredible economic costs, and take five long years of struggle, militarily, politically, economically, and diplomatically.

On the day Congress declared independence, a British fleet of some 130 warships and transports was moving toward New York. By the time the transports disembarked their troops, General Howe had a force of 32,000 well-trained, experienced British and Hessian troops to use in his assault on the New York City area. Opposing this magnificent force was a novice general and a mixture of volunteers of the Continental Army and state militia units totaling around 20,000, nearly all of whom were inexperienced, and many of whom were untrained in military discipline. The subsequent battles in and around New York City proved to be easy victories for the British, and devastating, demoralizing losses for Washington and the American troops. In fact, Washington was barely able to keep an army in the field after the fur stopped flying. Yet he and the army persevered.

Despite conspiracies against him in both the army and Congress over the succeeding years, Washington led the troops through many bad times and a few good. Volunteer militia units stood up when called and attempted to do their part.[299]

After a spectacular American military victory at Saratoga, New York, when the Americans defeated the British, and General Burgoyne and his entire army surrendered on October 17, 1777, France allied herself with America. She signed on to the fight against Britain in February 1778.

Meanwhile, Congress somehow found ways to keep the national government functioning. The individual state governments held up their ends as well. Then, on the afternoon of October 18, 1781, with the British band playing "The World Turned Upside Down," and the Redcoats bedecked in full uniform, General Cornwallis surrendered his army to the Americans.

When Prime Minister North was told of the surrender, he said, in effect, The War Is Lost. He believed Parliament would not fund another army to fight the Americans.[300]

Peace negotiations—and military conflicts—dragged on until 1783, when Britain formally recognized the United States of America.

Afterword

Then and Now

America's patriots were passionate in defense of their liberties. They were determined to preserve, or in some cases regain the rights they had enjoyed under the British Constitution in the decades prior to the French and Indian War. Many could not understand why British leaders were so unwilling to acknowledge those rights.

An important problem was that in the early- and mid-1770s, neither side realized its assumptions were not compatible with those of its adversary. Importantly, the rights under the British Constitution the patriots sought to protect differed from those parliamentary leaders believed existed. Fundamental to their differing interpretations were the matters of legislative representation and taxing authority.

In Britain, large segments of the population had no access to parliamentary representatives. Whole cities without representation in the House of Commons. To justify this remarkable blight on the nation's "representative" government, officials created the fiction of "virtual representation," arguing that a Member of Parliament represented not the residents of a particular district, but virtually all British citizens, no matter where they lived. This also meant that in the many "safe" districts, those where the government's candidate always won, an individual who resided outside the district—sometimes in a completely different region of the nation—was elected to that seat. Both of these ideas—population centers with no parliamentary representation, and House of Commons districts with a "representative" who did not reside in or, in fact, even tour that district—were completely foreign to American colonists.

The year 1619 was the date, and Jamestown, Virginia, the place where it all started. In that year the first legislative session in an English-American colony was held. Twenty men chosen from ten districts in the little colony comprised the lower house, eventually called the House of Burgesses.

Jamestown was the colony's only population center; clusters of farms and plantations were formed into districts (called hundreds) for representation at that first session. Voters in each "hundred" were to elect two of their neighbors to represent them at the legislative session in Jamestown. All landholders in each district apparently had the right to vote, for the directive establishing the legislative assembly said the delegates were "to bee respetially [i.e., especially] Chosen by the inhabitants."[301]

Authorities in London holding responsibility for general oversight of the Virginia colony wrote the directives for establishing this governing body, which the colony's governor then implemented. Clearly, those London officials did not realize they were creating a political institution that was outside English precedent. In one form or another as they came into being, all other American colonies followed the twin ideas that every populated area should have representation in the legislature's lower house, and those representatives should actually live in the district they represented.

Virginia's elected Burgesses were not timid. They pressed for, and soon won control of their internal affairs, affirming or denying certificates of election to the house, choosing their officers, and setting a code of conduct for members. They also maneuvered to gain authority to levy taxes, a project which finally bore fruit in 1666, when the governor formally acknowledged the lower house's exclusive right to determine tax policy. Another important legislative victory came when the Burgesses acquired the right to lay out new counties and authorize new local governments as the colony's population expanded. These were powers Britain's House of Commons did not possess.

Why bring up these matters after telling the story of colonists' revolutionary fight for liberty and independence? Because they demonstrate that for those patriot colonists, the Revolution was a conservative movement directed at protecting long-held political rights and liberties that Parliament was not only challenging but actually abrogating. In contrast, parliamentary leaders saw those same colonial rights as radical changes from their own domestic institutions and authority. In other words, they were ignorant of the colonies' long political and constitutional history.

The word "revolution" holds varied meanings and connotations. When one considers the French Revolution of 1789, the failed Eastern European revolutions of 1848, or the Russian Revolutions of 1917 and 1918, causes, driving forces, and consequences were vastly different from the American Revolution of 1776.

Leaders of these post-American Revolution movements demanded radical social and economic changes, as well as changes in governmental structure and organization. In some cases the radical leaders delivered on these demands when they grabbed power. French leaders even attempted to rename the days and change the length of the week. Both French and Russian leaders sought to outlaw organized religions instead of supporting religious liberty.

Compared with these extremes, the American Revolution, despite aspects of civil war and periodic outbursts of patriot oppression against loyalists, was directed at restoring individual liberty and preserving democratic political institutions that the patriots saw disappearing through oppressive, unconstitutional British policies and power. Economic changes resulting from the American Revolution stemmed from realities on the ground rather than from ideological dictates or systematic governmental restructuring.

Shifting from the eighteenth to the twenty-first century, one can see governmental actions and politicians' pronouncements stimulating citizen reaction and grass-roots organizations forming in protest to policies and pronouncements.

These modern protest groups, often calling themselves "Tea Parties," imply they have a spiritual connection to those who actually dumped East India Company tea into the Boston harbor in 1773.

Ties between those eighteenth-century patriots and twenty-first-century "tea party" organizations are easy to find—and seem quite legitimate. But a stronger connection can be made to the many Sons of Liberty groups that formed up and down the colonies starting in 1765 to protest Parliament's imposition of a stamp tax. They continued their work for a decade, until in 1774 and '75 broad-based local and colony-wide volunteer organizations took over governing responsibilities in each colony.

Sons of Liberty groups emerged in response to perceived British threats to individual liberties, both economic and political. There was no master organizer or dominant colonial authority stimulating local Sons' organizations. Rather, individuals in each community joined with like-minded colonists to form a patriot group. Leaders from one group might then write to groups in nearby communities, or, in unusual cases, to groups in adjacent colonies to inform them of pertinent details, to seek advice, or to coordinate activities. But each group acted independently.

When colonists realized the implications of the Massachusetts Government Act passed in 1774—that Parliament was claiming for itself the power to change colonial charters, and therefore colonial government as it saw fit—members of Sons of Liberty groups joined with other community and colony leaders to take control of local and colony-wide governments. These new action groups gradually became revolutionary governments. At that point, Sons of Liberty organizations had fulfilled their missions.

Twenty-first-century citizens formed Tea Party groups at the local level in response to perceived threats to individual liberties as a result of rapidly bloating budgets, phenomenal increases in government debt, and interference with individual and business freedom of actions through heavy-handed governmental regulation. These modern groups had no superior entity guiding them in their formation, in the internal management policies they established, or in the actions they pursued. They did communicate with like-minded groups in their area, in the state, and often on regional or national levels. But they maintained their independence. They also took political action, supporting candidates for office who espoused theories, policies, and values to the group's liking. They did not disband when elections were over, but often followed the actions and pronouncements of elected officials to see if they kept the promises they made during election campaigns. They also continued meeting on a regular basis and maintained relations with other groups locally, regionally, and nationally.

If governments, national, state, and local, reform their budgeting processes, establish and implement realistic plans for funding their debts, and pull back on stifling regulatory policies, will the modern Tea Party groups disband?

What is your assessment?

Of course, the generalizations given here, both historical and contemporary, are sufficiently broad so that one can shoot holes in them by using a finely sighted rifle. And for those who wish: fire away!

For the general reader who is looking for insight into a dramatic, critically important era in America's history rather than taking pot shots, I hope you have read the work with a critical eye, have raised questions with friends about fact and interpretation, and as a result, are walking away with a deeper understanding of how and why English colonists chose to become Americans, and how these eighteenth-century developments have relevance to twenty-first-century movements.

For Further Reading

Starting with the general era, two fine short histories are: Edmund S. Morgan's *The Birth of the Republic: 1763-89*, 3rd. edition, published by the University of Chicago Press, 1992; and Gordon S. Wood's *The American Revolution: A History*, revised edition, published by Modern Library in 2002. Dan Cook, a professional writer, offers a different perspective on the coming of the Revolution as well as the war itself, looking at these developments from London in *The Long Fuse: How England Lost the American Colonies, 1770-1785*. Atlantic Monthly Press published this work in 1995.

Focusing on the era leading to the Declaration of Independence, a relatively old, but still valuable work is: Lawrence Henry Gipson's *The Coming of the Revolution: 1763-1775*, Harper and Row, Publishers, 1954. Pauline Maier's first book, *From Resistance to Revolution*, Alfred A. Knopf, 1972, is carefully researched, insightful, and very readable. Parliamentary politics and policies are discussed in: Bernard Donoughue, *British Politics and the American Revolution*, London, Macmillan & Co., 1964; and Peter D. G. Thomas, *Tea Party to Independence*, Oxford, Clarendon Press, 1991.

Thomas S. Kidd has a pair of books which address the Great Awakening: *The Great Awakening A Brief History with Documents* includes a short narrative history of the movement, followed by excerpts of thirty-six documents, It was published in 2008 by Bedford/St. Martin's. Kidd's major work on the Awakening, published by Yale University Press in 2007, is: *The Great Awakening The Roots of Evangelical Christianity in Colonial America.*

Those interested in reviewing the Revolution's intellectual underpinnings will find they are involved in serious study. The best place to begin is in Bernard Bailyn's *The Ideological Origins of the American Revolution*, published in Cambridge, MA by the Belknap Press of Harvard University Press in 1967.

Two works giving considerable attention to the lead-up and events surrounding the Boston Tea Party are: Benjamin Woods Labaree, *The Boston Tea Party*, New York, Oxford University Press, 1964; and Benjamin L. Carp, *Defiance of the Patriots: The Boston Tea Party & The Making of America*, New Haven, Yale University Press, 2010. Chapter 6 of Carp's work: "The Destroyers at Griffin's Wharf," offers considerable detail in regard to the noble deed and those involved in it.

If you wish to study more deeply the politics and the ideology behind the decision to declare independence, as well as the Declaration of Independence itself, two essential works are: Carl L. Becker, *The Declaration of Independence*, New York, Vintage Books, 1942; and Pauline Maier, *American Scripture*, New York, Alfred A. Knopf, 1997.

Notes

[1] Abraham Lincoln, *Speeches and Writings 1859-1865*, Don E. Fehrenbacher, ed. (New York: Literary Classics of America, 1989), p. 209

[2] Francis S. Drake, *Tea Leaves* (Boston: A. O. Crane, 1884 [facsimile reprint by Singing Tree Press, 1970]), p. 319

[3] Fred Anderson, *The War That Made America* (New York: Penguin Books, 2005), p. 37-52

[4] Jerome R. Reich, *Colonial America*, 3rd. ed, (Englewood Cliffs, NJ: Prentice-Hall, 1994), p. 273

[5] Anderson, *The War That Made America*, p. 207-08

[6] Lawrence Henry Gipson, *The Coming of the Revolution* (New York: Harper and Row, 1954), p. 23; Reich, Colonial America, p. 280

[7] Charles M. Andrews, *The Colonial Background of the American Revolution*, [first published in 1924] (New Haven: Yale University Press, 1958) p. 130-133; Gordon S. Wood, The American Revolution (New York: New American Library, 2002), pp. 27-28

[8] Franklin B. Wickwire, *British Subministeres and Colonial America* (Princeton, NJ: Princeton University Press, 1966), pp. 102-03

[9] Ibid., 105-110; 190-193; Edmund S. & Helen M. Morgan, *The Stamp Act Crisis* (Chapel Hill: University of North Carolina Press, 1953), p. 70

[10] Ibid., 106

[11] Ibid., 112-13

[12] Ibid., 119-130; Merrill Jensen, *Founding of a Nation* (New York: Oxford University Press, 1968), pp. 63-64; Arthur M. Schlesinger, *Prelude to Independence* (New York: Vintage Books, 1965), pp. 33-34; Wesley S. Griswold, *The Night the Revolution Began* (Brattleboro, Vermont: The Stephen Green Press, 1972), p. 19

[13] Pauline Maier, *From Resistance to Revolution* (New York: Alfred A. Knopf, 1972) pp. 53-57; Trevor Colbourn, *The Lamp of Experience* (Chapel Hill, NC: University of North Carolina Press, 1965), pp. 63-65

[14] Morgan, *Stamp Act Crisis*, pp. 68-69

[15] Maier, *From Resistance to Revolution*, pp. 77-112

[16] Morgan, *Stamp Act Crisis*, p. 279

[17] Barbara W. Tuchman, *First Salute* (New York: Ballantine Books, 1988), p. 200

[18] Benjamin Franklin, *The Political Thought of Benjamin Franklin*, Ralph Ketcham, ed. (Indianapolis: Bobbs-Merrill Co., 1965), pp. 185-87

[19] Jensen, *Founding of a Nation*, p. 255

[20] Ibid., pp. 288-91

[21] Gipson, *Coming of the Revolution*, pp. 209-10; Edmund Cody Burnett, *The Continental Congress* (New York: W.W. Norton, 1941), p. 16

[22] Schlesinger, *Prelude to Independence*, pp. 154-55; Lawrence Henry Gipson, *Triumphant Empire* (New York: Alfred A. Knopf, 1965), pp. 24-37

[23] Don Cook, *The Long Fuse* (New York: Atlantic Monthly Press, 1995), pp. 165-68

[24] Brian Gardner, *The East India Company* (New York: Dorset Press, 1961), ch. 1

[25] Lucy Sutherland, *The East India Company in Eighteeth-Century Politics* (Oxford: Oxford University Press, 1952), p. 138n

[26] R. J. White, *The Age of George III* (New York: Walker & Co., 1966), pp. 118-19

[27] Cook, *The Long Fuse*, pp. 115-16

[28] Theodore Draper, *A Struggle for Power* (New York: Times Books, 1966), p. 390

[29] Ibid., 390-91

[30] Arthur M. Schlesinger, *Colonial Merchants and the American Revolution* (Forge Village, MA: Atheneum, 1968), pp. 248-51

[31] Jensen, *Founding of a Nation*, pp. 434-35

[32] Sutherland, *East India Co. in 18th Century Politics*, pp. 249-50

[33] Ibid., 241

[34] Ibid., 251-52

[35] Bernard Donoughue, B*ritish Politics and the American Revolution* (London: Macmillan & Co., 1964), p. 21

[36] Benjamin Woods Labaree, *The Boston Tea Party* (Boston: Northeastern University Press, 1964), pp. 66-68

[37] Ibid., 70-71

[38] Ira Stoll, *Samuel Adams A Life* (New York: Free Press, 2008), p. 106

[39] Jensen, *Founding of a Nation*, p. 437; Donoughue, *British Politics and the American Revolution*, p. 22

[40] Ibid., 23

[41] Drake, *Tea Leaves*, pp. 199-215

[42] Ibid., 201, 216, 218; Labaree, *Boston Tea Party*, p. 77

[43] Gipson, *Triumphant Empire*, pp. 72-73

[44] Drake, *Tea Leaves*, pp. 258, 267, 272-282

[45] The quotation in Edward's statement is from Second Corinthians, Chapter 5, verse 17, Jonathan Edwards, *A Faithful Narrative of the Surprising Work of God in the Great Awakening*, as printed in *The Great Awakening A Brief History with Documents*, ed. by Thomas S. Kidd, (Chicago, Bedford/St. Martins, 2008), p. 36

[46] Jonathan Edwards, "Justification by Faith Alone," in *The Great Awakening Documents Illustrating the Crisis and Its Consequences*, ed. by Alan Heimert and Perry Miller (Indianapolis: Bobbs-Merrill Company, Inc., 1967), p. 9

[47] "The Letter of Paul to the Romans," Chapter 9, verses 30-33; Chapter 10 verses 10-13, *The Holy Bible*, English Standard Version (Wheaton, Illinois: Crossway Bibles, 2004), p. 1203

[48] Thomas Kidd, *The Great Awakening: The Roots of Evangelical Christianity in America* (New Haven: Yale University Press, 2007), p. 40

[49] Edwin Scott Gaustad, *The Great Awakening in New England* (Chicago: Quadrangle Paperback, 1968), p. 121

[50] Wood, *The American Revolution*, p. 16; Rhys Isaac, *The Transformation of Virginia* (Chapel Hill: University of North Carolina Press, 1982), pp. 162-63

[51] Colin Bonwick, *The American Revolution* (Charolettesville, VA: University Press of Virginia, 1991), p. 63

[52] Kidd, *The Great Awakening A Brief History With Documents*, pp. 60-64

[53] Ibid., pp. 72-74

[54] Gaustad, *The Great Awakening*, p. 103

[55] Heimert and Perry, *The Great Awakening*, p. xv; Isaac, *The Transformation of Virginia*, p. 266n

[56] Bonwick, *The American Revolution*, p. 69

[57] Labaree, *Boston Tea Party*, p. 262

[58] Jensen, *Founding of a Nation*, p. 40

[59] Ibid., 155-56

[60] White, T*he Age of George III*, pp. 65-69

[61] Jensen, *Founding of a Nation*, pp. 156-57

[62] Bernard Bailyn, *Ideological Origins of the American Revolution* (Cambridge: The Belknap Press, 1967), pp. 110-12; Jensen, *Founding of a Nation*, p. 317

[63] Ibid., 318

[64] Bailyn, *Ideological Origins of the American Revolution*, p. 115

[65] Ibid., 116

[66] Jensen, *Founding of a Nation*, pp. 317-20

[67] Schlesinger, *Prelude to Independedence*, p. 35

[68] Jack P. Greene, *Quest for Power* (Chapel Hill: University of North Carolina Press, 1963), pp. 403-16

[69] Colbourn, *The Lamp of Experience*, p. 19

[70] David L. Jacobson (ed.) *The English Libertarian Heritage* (Indianapolis: Bobbs-Merrill Co., 1965), pp. lxii, 1-2

[71] Bailyn, *Ideological Origins of the American Revolution*, p. 36; Jacobson, *English Libertarian Heritage*, p. xxv, n

[72] Ibid., xxvii, xlvii-lvii; Bailyn, *Ideological Origins of the American Revolution*, pp. 44, 53; Colbourn, *Lamp of Experience*, pp. 200-230

[73] Ibid., 78

[74] Bailyn, *Ideological Origins of the American Revolution*, p. 56

[75] Ibid., 66-69. 71-74

[76] Ibid., 277; Labaree, *Boston Tea Party*, p. 115

[77] Anderson, *The War That Made America*, pp. 242-44

[78] Aubrey C. Land, *The Dulanys of Maryland* (Baltimore: The Johns Hopkins Press, 1965), p. 263

[79] Ibid.

[80] Ibid.

[81] Ibid., 264

[82] Ibid., 264-64; Morgan, *The Stamp Act Crisis*, pp. 105-110

[83] Ibid., 180-204

[84] Ibid., 286

[85] Ibid., 203

[86] Schlesinger, *Prelude to Independence*, pp. 88, 88n, 89; Jensen, *Founding of a Nation*, pp. 241-42; Forrest McDonald, ed., *Empire and Nation: Letters from a Farmer in Pennsylvania, John Dickinson...* (Englewood Cliffs, NJ: Prentice-Hall, 1962), pp. xii-xiii

[87] Ibid., 43, 44, 81n, 80; Colbourn, *Lamp of Experience*, p. 110

[88] Schlesinger, *Prelude to Independence*, p. 89; Carl Becker, *The Declaration of Independence* (New York: Vintage Books, 1942), pp. 96-97

[89] Ibid., 98-100

[90] Bailyn, *Ideological Origins*, p. 114

[91] Schlesinger, *Prelude to Independence*, pp. 100-110

[92] Jensen, *Founding of a Nation*, p. 352

[93] Ibid., 225-26

[94] Schlesinger, *Prelude to Independence*, p. 87

[95] Jensen, *Founding of a Nation*, p. 249

[96] Ibid., 249-50

[97] Ibid., 250

[98] Donoughue, *British Politics and the American Revolution*, pp. 114-15

[99] Gipson, *Coming of the Revolution*, p. 197

[100] Jensen, *Founding of a Nation*, p. 253

[101] Schlesinger, *Prelude to Independence*, pp. 17-18; Jensen, *Founding of a Nation*, pp. 253-54

[102] Ibid., 258-59, 260-62

[103] Ibid., 260; Schlesinger, *Prelude to Independence*, p. 36

[104] Maier, *Resistance to Revolution*, pp. 232-33; Donoughue, *British Politics*, p. 7

[105] Schlesinger, *Prelude to Independence*, p. 86

[106] Gipson, *Coming of the Revolution*, pp. 187-88; Jensen, *Founding of a Nation*, pp. 281-87

[107] Dirk Hoerder, "Boston Leaders and Boston Crowds, 1765-1776," in *The American Revolution*, Alfred F. Young, ed., (De Kalb, Ill., Northern Illinois University Press, 1976), pp. 260-61; Labaree, *The Boston Tea Party*, p. 138; Schlesinger, *Colonial Merchants and the American Revolution*, pp. 284-86

[108] Stoll, *Samuel Adams A Life*, p. 115

[109] Gipson, *The Coming of the Revolution*, p. 220; "Reminisces of the Tea Party," in *Chronicles of the American Revolution*, ed. by Alden T.

Vaughan (New York, Grosset & Dunlap, 1965), pp. 67-68; Marc Engal, *Mighty Empire* (Ithaca, Cornell University Press, 1988), p. 354

[110] John C. Miller, *Sam Adams: Pioneer in Propaganda* (Stanford, CA: Stanford University Press, 1936), pp. 293-94

[111] Vaughan, ed., *Chronicles of the American Revolution*, p. 68

[112] Vaughan, ed., *Chronicles of the American Revolution*, p. 68; Labaree, *The Boston Tea Party*, pp. 141-45; Drake, *Tea Leaves*, pp. XCII- CLXXII; Griswold, *The Night the Revolution Began*, pp. 141-143; Benjamin L. Carp, *Defiance of the Patriots* (New Haven, CT., Yale University Press, 2010), pp. 234-239

[113] Miller, *Sam Adams*, p. 293

[114] Labaree, *The Boston Tea Party*, pp. 141, 144

[115] Donald Barr Chidsey, *The Great Separation* (New York: Crown Publishers, 1965), p. 5

[116] Griswold, *The Night the Revolution Began*, p. 141; Esther Forbes, *Paul Revere* (Boston: Houghton Mifflin Co., 1942), pp. 200, 206-07; Peter D. G. Thomas, *Tea Party to Independence* (Oxford: Clarendon Press, 1991), p. 22

[117] Schlesinger, *Colonial Merchants and the American Revolution*, p. 301; Donoughue, *British Politics and the American Revolution*, pp. 29-30

[118] Esmond Wright, ed., *The Fire of Liberty* (London, The Folio Society, 1983), pp. 11-12

[119] John Adams, *The Adams Papers*, L. H. Butterfield, ed. (New York: Atheneum, 1964), II, pp. 85-86

[120] Labaree, *Boston Tea Party*, pp. 146-47

[121] Drake, *Tea Leaves*, pp. 309-320

[122] Thomas, *Tea Party to Independence*, pp. 33-34; 46

[123] Schlesinger, *Colonial Merchants and the American Revolution*, p. 302n

[124] Labaree, *Boston Tea Party*, p. 77; Thomas, *Tea Party to Independence*, p. 11

[125] Schlesinger, *Colonial Merchants*, p. 281; Jensen, Founding of a Nation, p. 441

[126] Eric Foner, "Tom Paine's Republic: Radical Ideology and Social Change," in The American Revolution, Young, ed., pp. 194-96; Schlesinger, Colonial Merchants and the American Revolution, pp. 441-42; Labaree, Boston Tea Party, pp. 97-103

[127] Thomas, *Tea Party to Independence*, p. 23

[128] Vaughan, ed., *Chronicles of the American Revolution*, pp. 68-72

[129] Jensen, *Founding of a Nation*, p. 444; Bernard Mason, *Road to Independence* (Lexington: University of Kentucky Press, 1966), pp. 8-18

[130] Ibid., 19-22

[131] Ibid., 20-21

[132] John Richard Alden, *The South in the Revolution* (Baton Rouge: Louisiana University Press: 1957), pp. 166-69

[133] Maier, *From Resistance to Revolution*, pp. 298, 298n-300n; Schlesinger, *Colonial Merchants and the American Revolution*, pp. 265, 295-98

[134] Labaree, *Boston Tea Party*, pp. 150-151

[135] J. Thomas Scharf, *History of Maryland, 3 vols.*, Fascsimile reprint of the 1879 edition, (Hatboro, PA: Tradition Press, 1976), II, 159-161, 161n

[136] Morgan, *The Stamp Act Crisis*, pp. 123-25

[137] John Richard Alden, *The American Revolution* (New York: Harper & Row, 1954), pp. 5-6

[138] Jensen, *Founding of a Nation*, p. 439

[139] Ibid., 437; Schlesinger, *Colonial Merchants and the American Revolution*, pp. 285-86

[140] Greene, *Quest for Power,* pp. 380-87; Draper, *Struggle for Power*, pp. 291-95

[141] Maier, *From Resistance to Revolution*, pp. 8, 11-12; Jensen, *Founding of a Nation*, pp. 425-30

[142] Thomas, *Tea Party to Independence*, pp. 29-32; Donoughue, *British Politics and the American Revolution*, pp. 48-54

[143] Ibid., 55-59, 62

[144] Ibid., 63

[145] Ibid., 64-65

[146] Thomas, *Tea Party to Independence*, pp. 30-31

[147] Donoughue, *British Politics and the American Revolution*, p. 63, 64-65

[148] Thomas, *Tea Party to Independence*, pp. 38-41

[149] Donoughue, *British Politics and the American Revolution*, pp. 49-50

[150] Thomas, *Tea Party to Independence*, pp. 46-47

[151] Ibid., 48-50

[152] Ibid., 50

[153] Ibid., 55

[154] Ibid., 59

[155] Donoughue, *British Politics and the American Revolution*, pp. 84-85

[156] Ibid., 87-88

[157] Thomas, pp. 70-71

[158] Ibid., 71-72

[159] Ibid., 79-82, 84-85

[160] Alden, *The American Revolution*, pp. 11, 46

[161] Fred Anderson, *Crucible of War* (New York: Alfred A. Knopf, 2000), pp. 565-66, 730-31

[162] Thomas, *Tea Party to Independence*, p. 90; Donoughue, *British Politics and the American Revolution*, pp. 109-10

[163] Ibid., 110-11; Gipson, *The Coming of the Revolution*, p. 226; Jensen, *Founding of a Nation*, p. 396; Thomas, *Tea Party to Independence*, p. 93

[164] Donoughue, *British Politics and the American Revolution*, pp. 113-120

[165] Thomas, *Tea Party to Independence*, p. 100

[166] Schlesinger, *Prelude to Independence*, p. 199

[167] Donoughue, *British Politics and the American Revolution*, pp. 121-22; Thomas, *Tea Party to Independence*, pp. 104-05

[168] Ibid., 105-06

[169] Ibid., 88-117

[170] Labaree, *Boston Tea Party*, p. 222

[171] Schlesinger, *Prelude to Independence*, p. 199

[172] Thomas Jefferson, *Writings*, Complied by Merrill D. Peterson (New York: Library Company of America, 1976), pp. 105-22

[173] Ibid., 105

[174] Ibid., 105, 106, 118-19

[175] Ibid., 117

[176] Ibid., 110

[177] Ibid., 111

[178] Ibid., 120-21

[179] Gipson, *Triumphant Empire*, p. 295

[180] Miller, *Sam Adams: Pioneer in Propaganda*, p. 302

[181] Ibid., 302-04

[182] Ibid., 305-06; Schlesinger, *Colonial Merchants and the American Revolution*, pp. 326-28

[183] Ibid., 342-47; 356-58; 359-79

[184] Thomas, *Tea Party to Independence*, p. 120; Miller, *Sam Adams*, p. 308

[185] Stoll, *Samuel Adams: A Life*, p. 127; Thomas, *Tea Party to Independence*, p. 121; Mark Puls, *Samuel Adams* (New York: Palgrave Macmillan, 2006), pp. 154-55

[186] Jensen, *Founding of a Nation*, p. 475

[187] Labaree, *Boston Tea Party*, pp. 233-34; Schlesinger, *Colonial Merchants and the American Revolution*, pp. 362-63

[188] Jensen, *Founding of a Nation*, pp. 476-77

[189] Schlesinger, *Colonial Merchants and the American Revolution*, pp. 368-70; Thomas, *Tea Party to Independence*, p. 127

[190] George Washington, *Writings*, selected by John Rhodehamel (New York: The Library of America, 1997), p. 158; Puls, *Samuel Adams*, p. 159

[191] Thomas, *Tea Party to Independence*, p. 128; Christopher Gadsden, *The Writings of Christopher Gadsden*, Richard Walsh, ed. (Columbia, S.C.: University of South Carolina Press, 1966), pp. 100-101

[192] Schlesinger, *Colonial Merchants and the American Revolution*, p. 341

[193] Labaree, *Boston Tea Party*, pp. 230-31

[194] Jensen, *Founding of a Nation*, p. 480; Schlesinger, *Colonial Merchants and the American Revolution*, pp. 351-56

[195] Mason, *The Road to Independence*, pp. 25-35; Schlesinger, *Colonial Merchants and the American Revolution*, pp. 339-40

[196] Thomas, *Tea Party to Independence*, p. 126

[197] Labaree, *Boston Tea Party*, p. 240; Schlesinger, *Colonial Merchants and the American Revolution*, p. 327

[198] Jensen, *Founding of a Nation*, pp. 516, 518; Schlesinger, *Colonial Merchants and the American Revolution*, pp. 379-84

[199] Thomas, *Tea Party to Independence*, pp. 86, 149; Donoughue, *British Politics and the American Revolution*, pp. 201-02

[200] Jensen, *Founding of a Nation*, pp. 551-53

[201] Schlesinger, *Colonial Merchants and the American Revolution*, pp. 386-88; Jensen, *Founding of a Nation*, pp. 550-556

[202] Donoughue, *British Politics and the American Revolution*, pp. 117, 181-88

[203] Gipson, *Triumphant Empire*, p. 270

[204] Donoughue, *British Politics and the American Revolution*, pp. 184, 200; Gipson, *Triumphant Empire*, p. 272n

[205] Thomas, *Tea Party to Independence*, pp. 148-49

[206] Donoughue, p. 198, 199; Thomas, *Tea Party to Independence*, pp. 148-49

[207] Adams, *Adams Papers*, II, p. 101

[208] Ibid., 106; Miller, *Sam Adams*, p. 318; Puls, *Samuel Adams*, pp. 158-59

[209] Miller, *Sam Adams*, pp. 318-19; Burnett, *Continental Congress*, p. 31

[210] Ibid., 33-34

[211] Jensen, *Founding of a Nation*, p. 490; Burnett, *The Continental Congress*, pp. 33-34

34; Schlesinger, *Colonial Merchants*, p. 411

[212] Adams, *Adams Papers*, II, pp. 126, 135

[213] Ibid., 156

[214] Burnett, *Continental Congress*, p. 38

[215] Ibid., 41

[216] Jensen, *Founding of a Nation*, pp. 492-94

[217] Burnett, *Continental Congress*, pp. 41-42; Jensen, *Founding of a Nation*, pp. 492-96; 502-03

[218] Ibid., 495-96

[219] Puls, *Samuel Adams*, p. 161; Burnett, *Continental Congress*, pp. 42-44; Miller, *Sam Adams*, pp. 323-24; Jensen, *Founding of a Nation*, pp. 495-96; Thomas, *Tea Party to Independence*, p. 158

[220] Schlesinger, *Colonial Merchants*, pp. 413-14

[221] Adams, *Papers*, II, pp. 242-44; Burnett, *Continental Congress*, pp. 48-50

[222] Ibid., Jensen, *Founding of a Nation*, pp. 499-500

[223] Burnett, *Continental Congress*, pp. 50-58

[224] Schlesinger, *Colonial Merchants,* pp. 412-430

[225] Jensen, *Founding of a Nation*, p. 504; Adams, *Papers*, II, pp. 152n-153n

[226] Schlesinger, *Colonial Merchants and the American Revolution*, pp. 421-23

[227] The text of the Association is in Ibid., 607-613

[228] Burnett, *Continental Congress*, pp. 54-57

[229] Thomas, *Tea Party to Independence*, pp. 154-55

[230] Ibid., 137-38, 158-59; Donoughue, *British Politics and the American Revolution*, p. 208n; Burnett, *Continental Congress*, pp. 47-48

[231] Thomas, *Tea Party to Independence*, p. 169

[232] Alden, *American Revolution*, pp. 63-64; Thomas, *Tea Party to Independence*, pp. 185-86

[233] Ibid., 188

[234] Jensen, *Founding a Nation*, pp. 575-76

[235] Ibid., 576

[236] Schlesinger, *Prelude to Independence*, pp. 232-34; Wood, *The American Revolution*, pp. 53-54

[237] Burnett, *Continental Congress*, pp. 65, 66

[238] Jensen, *Founding of a Nation*, p. 603

[239] Donoughue, *British Politics and the American Revolution*, p. 248n

[240] Jensen, *Founding of a Nation*, p. 581

[241] Donoughue, *British Politics and the American Revolution*, pp. 249, 250

[242] Burnett, *Continental Congress*, p. 68; Christopher Ward, *The War of the Revolution*, two volumes, edited by John R. Alden (New York: Macmillan Co., 1952), I, pp. 52-55; Alden, *American Revolution*, p. 26; Alden, *South in the Revolution*, pp. 192-94

[243] Jensen, *Founding of a Nation*, p. 606

[244] Ibid., 552-55; Alden, *American Revolution*, pp. 11-14; Schlesinger, *Colonial Merchants and the American Revolution*, pp. 473-78, 535-36, 541-54

[245] Ward, *War of the Revolution*, I, pp. 54-55; Burnett, *Continental Congress*, pp. 71, 74

[246] Dave Palmer, *George Washington and Benedict Arnold* (Washington, DC: Regnery Publishing, 2006), pp. 81-82; Ward, *War of the Revolution*, I, pp. 63-72

[247] Ibid., 70-71; Palmer, *George Washington and Benedict Arnold*, pp. 90, 94

[248] Burnett, *Continental Congress*, p. 68

[249] Ibid., 68, 108-09

[250] Thomas, *Tea Party to Independence*, p. 242; Ward, *War of the Revolution*, I, pp. 73-74, 78

[251] Thomas, *Tea Party to Independence*, pp. 254, 258; Ward, *War of the Revolution*, I, pp. 73-98

[252] Burnett, *Continental Congress*, p. 71; Alden, *American Revolution*, p. 29; Maier, *From Resistance to Revolution*, p. 40

[253] Palmer, *George Washington and Benedict Arnold*, p. 97, 98; Burnett, *Continental Congress*, pp. 75-76, 85-86

[254] Ibid., 71-74; 93-94

[255] Colbourn, *Lamp of Experience*, p. 117; Gipson, *Triumphant Empire*, p. 338

[256] Burnett, *Continental Congress*, pp. 124-26

[257] Becker, *Declaration of Independence*, p. 127; Colbourn, *Lamp of Experience*, p. 117

[258] Gipson, *Triumphant Empire*, pp. 338-39

[259] Thomas, *Tea Party to Independence*, p. 263

[260] Gipson, *Triumphant Empire*, p. 339; Thomas, *Tea Party*, pp. 264-65

[261] Donoughue, *British Politics and the American Revolution*, pp. 215-16, 221-22,

224-26; Thomas, *Tea Party to Independence*, pp. 297-302, 303-04, 315-19, 323-25, 329; Burnett, *Continental Congress*, pp. 199-204

[262] Ward, *War of the Revolution*, I, pp. 133-34

[263] Ibid., II, 845-46

[264] Ibid., 847-49

[265] Ibid., 849

[266] Alden, *American Revolution*, pp. 77-78; Maier, *Resistance to Revolution*, p. 257; Pauline Maier, *American Scripture* (New York: Alfred A. Knopf, 1997), pp. 38-39; Thomas, *Tea Party to Independence*, pp. 305-06

[267] Alden, *American Revolution*, p. 77 & 77n

[268] Thomas Paine, *Common Sense*, introduction by Isaac Kramnick (London: Penguin Books, 1976), pp. 25-28

[269] Ibid., 28

[270] Ibid., 65

[271] Ibid., 73, 81

[272] Ibid., 92

[273] Ibid., 87-88, 91

[274] Maier, *American Scripture*, p. 34

[275] Paine, *Common Sense*, p. 29; Joseph Perry, "Diary of Rev. Joseph Perry," ed. by James Van Ness, *Proceedings of the Bostonian Society*, Boston, MA, January 15, 1963, p. 33

[276] Bernard Bailyn, *Faces of Revolution* (New York: Vintage Books, 1990), p. 84

[277] Maier, *American Scripture*, p. 28

[278] Becker, *Declaration of Independence*, p. 129; Burnett, *Continental Congress*, p. 157

[279] Maier, *From Resistance to Revolution*, p. 211; Maier, *American Scripture*, p. 37

[280] Adams, *Adams Papers*, II, pp. 238-40, 240n-241n; Burnett, *Continental Congress*, pp. 158-61; Maier, *American Scripture*, pp. 37-38

[281] Alden, *South in the Revolution*, p. 210-11

[282] Burnett, *Continental Congress*, pp. 167, 168-69; Alden, *South in the Revolution*, p. 212; Maier, *American Scripture*, p. 49

[283] Ibid., 48

[284] Burnett, *Continental Congress*, p. 171

[285] Ibid., 171-73

[286] Maier, *American Scripture*, p. 42

[287] Ibid., 232

[288] Ibid., 217-23, 225-34

[289] Ibid., 76

[290] Burnett, *Continental Congress*, pp. 176-84, 191

[291] Ibid., 184-88

[292] White, *Age of George III*, p. 110

[293] Becker, *Declaration of Independence*, pp. 187-190; Greene, *Quest of Power*, pp. 178-79

[294] Becker, *Declaration of Independence*, p. 190

[295] Ibid., 190-91

[296] Ibid., 192

[297] Ibid., 192-93; Jensen, *Founding of a Nation*, p. 701; Burnett, *Continental Congress*, pp. 213-14

[298] Schlesinger, *Prelude to Independence*, pp. 282-83; Jensen, *Founding of a Nation*, p. 702

[299] Ward, *War of the Revolution*, I, pp. 207-209

[300] Ibid., 538, 540, 894

[301] Warren M. Billings, John E. Selby, Thad W. Tate, *Colonial Virginia*, (White Plains, NY: kto press, 1986), pp. 42-43; 70-71; Warren M. Billings, ed., *The Old Dominion in the Seventeenth Century*, (Chapel Hill: The University of North Carolina Press, 1975), p. 38